DEEP LEARNING

DL1943 CHEATSHEET

DL/AI/ML RESEARCH, ENGINEERING, OPTIMIZATION & SYSTEM DESIGN

Not just another AI book.

Because there is enough theoretical knowledge.

We give you the real research and engineering knowledge you lack. No AI will replace you if you have this skill. For theoretical knowledge, search algorithms were enough.

Edition v1.0

Calder Reed 🖐 Chen Hui Fang

1

DEEP LEARNING ENGINEER

INTRODUCTION

This book will change your Deep Learning skills forever. Read it now to level up your future.

This book "**Deep Learning: DL1943 Cheatsheet: DL/AI/ML Research, Engineering, Optimization & System Design**" is the only book you need to master Deep Learning (DL) concepts. The focus is on research and engineering ideas.

This is a **cheatsheet** *just like* **distilled datasets**.

You do not need to read 1000s of pages. Just 150 pages is enough to revise the cutting-edge Deep Learning engineering and research ideas.

This book include:

- Chapters covering all core concepts in DL research, engineering and optimization including:
    - Basic concepts like Perceptron, Gradient Descent
    - All basic terms like epoch, topK and basic ops like MaxPool
    - Concepts to **run algorithms in parallel in GPU and CPU**
    - Core techniques like **INT8 Quantization**
    - **Deep Learning System Design** (with examples)
    - **Numerical Analysis** concepts like INT32 IEEE754, emulating FP64 using FP32.
    - Model architectures from MLP to CNN to LLM.
    - **Optimization techniques** across:
        - Assembly instructions like **AVX512 VNNI**
        - Algorithmic optimizations for DL operations like **MatMul**
        - Graph level operations
    - and much more.

- Each chapter is a **CHEATSHEET**. It includes to-the-point explanation and relevant code snippets.
- Each concept can be covered quickly in at most 4 minutes.
- Over 350 DL/AI concepts have been covered.

With this, you will be able to crack any Deep Learning Coding Interview easily.

After reading this book, you will:

- Master Deep Learning/ Artificial Intelligence.
- Clear interviews for full-time positions at high-tech companies. Good enough for:
  - Software Engineer 2/3, Machine Learning or Senior Software Engineer, AI/ML GenAI or ML Analyst at **Google** (L3/L4/L5)
  - Software Engineer, Machine Learning (E4/E5/E6) at **Meta**
  - Senior Deep Learning Systems Software Engineer - AI or AI Developer Technology Engineer at **NVIDIA**
  - Kernel Software Engineer - AI/ML GPU or Senior Machine Learning Software Engineer at **AMD**
  - Lead Engineer, Senior-C/C++, machine learning at **Qualcomm**
  - Machine Learning Engineer at **Microsoft** (Level 60 to 66)
  - And much more.

This book is for:

- Students and developers preparing for Coding Interviews specifically for Machine Learning/Deep Learning/GenAI positions.
- Experienced developers who wanted to revise their Deep Learning skills.
- Students who need a coding sheet to revise DL/AI/ML topics quickly.

Get started with this book and change the equation of your career.

 DL1943 Cheatsheet: Deep Learning ©

Book: **Deep Learning: DL1943 Cheatsheet: DL/AI/ML Research, Engineering, Optimization & System Design**

Authors (2): Calder Reed, Chen Hui Fang

Published: February 2025 (Edition 1)

ISBN: 9798310930803

Pages: 148

Available on Amazon as e-Book, Paperback and Hardcover.

TABLE OF CONTENTS

Matrix Multiplication [GEMM].. 8

Convolution operation [1989] 15

Deep Learning System Design.. 20

INT8 Quantization 38

GPU Workload Parallelization... 44

CPU architecture (for parallel workload) 62

DL Software Stack 64

DL breakthroughs Timeline 66

Deep Learning model list [Applications].. 67

Training & Inference time of DL models 74

Perceptron [1943]... 76

Linear layer (nn.linear)... 78

Perceptron with step function 79

Single Layer Neural Network 81

Multi-Layer Perception (MLP) / Neural Network [1958] 82

RNN & LSTM [1982, 1997] 86

Transformer Neural Network [2017] 90

Attention [2017].. 93

BERT [2018] 95

LLM [2018] 99

AlexNet [2012] 101

ResNet50 [2015] 103

Training your model.. 106

Inference 107

Datatypes (dtype) in Deep Learning 108

FP32 IEEE754 Floating Point 111

Emulate FP64 using FP32 114

FP8 in DL.. 118

Hardware platforms for Deep Learning 119

Accuracy 121

Loss... 124

Loss landscape 127

Gradient descent... 128

Backpropagation [1975].. 129

Preparing dataset for training.. 130

Bias Variance 131

Performance metrics 133

Activation Functions 135

MaxPool and AvgPool 137

Fully Connected Layer (FC) 138

Dropout [1990] 139

Regularization techniques 140

Other core DL operations.. 142

Convolution Neural Network (CNN) [1995] 143

CONCLUDING NOTE 147

Matrix Multiplication [GEMM]

The most fundamental mathematical operation in all DL models.

Understanding and optimizing this is like winning half of the battle.

This mathematical operation lies at the heart of Deep Learning. It is correct to say that the entire field is based on understanding and applying the potential of this fundamental operation.

Dot product

Same as multiplication but handling multiple data points together.

- Given 2 arrays, multiply i^{th} element of first array with i^{th} element of second array and the product is the ith value of the output array.

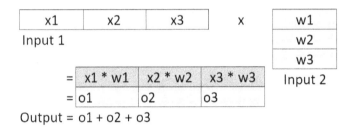

Matrix **Multiplication** is the core operation in Deep Learning.

Given a matrix A of size MxK and B of size KxN, the output is of size MxN.

(i, j) element is the dot product of ith row of matrix A and j^{th} column of matrix B.

Remember: **"First row by first column"**, **"First row by second column"**, ...,
"second row by first column", **"second row by second column"**, ...

a1	a2	a3
a4	a5	a6
a7	a8	a9
a10	a11	a12

Input (say image)

b1	b4
b2	b5
b3	b6

2nd Input (say weight)

x

c1	c2
c3	c4
c5	c6
c7	c8

Output

c1	=	a1 * b1 + a2 * b2 + a3 * b3

The time complexity of brute force approach for Matrix Multiplication is **O(MNK)**. Matrix Multiplication is referred to as **MatMul**.

Standard arithmetic libraries provide **GEMM** methods for such operation.

GEMM = Generalized matrix multiplication

GEMM is a highly optimized method and CPUs and GPUs have in-built efficient support for them.

The equation of GEMM is:

Output = α AB + β C

- A is a matrix of size MxK
- B is a matrix of size KxN
- Output and C is a matrix of size MxN
- α, β are scalar values.

GEMM is considered as the **most fundamental operation of Deep Learning**.

It is used in majority of the critical operations like Convolution, Fully Connected layer, Dot Product/ Self Attention, Layer/ Batch Normalization, Backpropagation Gradient.

9

Optimized Implementation of MatMul is an important skill for DL engineers.

Brute force implementation:

```
for (int i = 0; i < M; i++) {
    for (int j = 0; j < N; j++) {
        for (int k = 0; k < K; k++) {
            // Poor cache reuse
            C[i][j] += A[i][k] * B[k][j];
        }
    }
}
```

Optimized GEMM Using Tiling (16×K Blocking)

Tiling (or blocking) divides matrices into smaller submatrices (tiles) to ensure efficient cache utilization and minimize memory bandwidth bottlenecks. Steps:

- Break matrix C into smaller tiles of 16×K
- Process one tile at a time, keeping it in L1/L2 cache

```
// Tiling
const int TILE_SIZE = 16;

for (int i = 0; i < M; i += TILE_SIZE) {
    for (int j = 0; j < N; j += TILE_SIZE) {
        for (int k = 0; k < K; k += TILE_SIZE) {

            // Process 16×K block at a time
            for (int ii = i; ii < i + TILE_SIZE; ii++) {
                for (int jj = j; jj < j + TILE_SIZE; jj++) {
                    for (int kk = k; kk < k + TILE_SIZE; kk++) {
                        C[ii][jj] += A[ii][kk] * B[kk][jj];
                    }
                }
            }

        }
    }
}
```

```
}
```

Why 16×K Blocking?

16xK means each tile has 16 rows of A and K columns of B.

16 is chosen because:

- Fits well in CPU SIMD registers (AVX512 = 16 floats in one vector).
- Efficient cache line utilization (aligned to 64-byte cache lines).
- K is chosen based on L2 cache size.

Benefit: Higher cache reuse, fewer memory accesses, better vectorization.

Using Prefetching in GEMM

- Load next tile into L1/L2 cache while computing current tile.
- Use _mm_prefetch() for explicit software prefetching.

Memory accesses are hidden, resulting in better throughput.

```
// Prefetch
for (int i = 0; i < M; i += TILE_SIZE) {
    for (int j = 0; j < N; j += TILE_SIZE) {
        for (int k = 0; k < K; k += TILE_SIZE) {

            // Prefetch next tile of A and B into cache
            _mm_prefetch((char*)&A[i][k + TILE_SIZE],
_MM_HINT_T0);
            _mm_prefetch((char*)&B[k + TILE_SIZE][j],
_MM_HINT_T0);

            // Process current tile
            for (int ii = i; ii < i + TILE_SIZE; ii++) {
                for (int jj = j; jj < j + TILE_SIZE; jj++) {
                    for (int kk = k; kk < k + TILE_SIZE; kk++) {
                        C[ii][jj] += A[ii][kk] * B[kk][jj];
                    }
                }
            }
        }
    }
}
```

```
            }
        }
      }
  }
```

Software Pipelining in GEMM

- Overlaps memory loads with computation.
- Instead of waiting for data fetch to complete, execute independent operations.
- Can be done manually (reordering loops) or automatically (compiler optimizations).

Break computation into multiple stages:

- Load A, B into registers.
- Compute C = A × B.
- Store result of C back to memory.
- Start loading next tile (overlap compute with memory fetch).

```
// Pipelining
for (int i = 0; i < M; i += TILE_SIZE) {
    for (int j = 0; j < N; j += TILE_SIZE) {
        for (int k = 0; k < K; k += TILE_SIZE) {

            __m512 a_tile, b_tile, c_tile;

            for (int ii = i; ii < i + TILE_SIZE; ii++) {
                for (int kk = k; kk < k + TILE_SIZE; kk++) {

                    // Prefetch next A block before using it
                    _mm_prefetch((char*)&A[ii][kk + TILE_SIZE],
_MM_HINT_T0);

                    // Load current A block
                    a_tile = _mm512_load_ps(&A[ii][kk]);

                    for (int jj = j; jj < j + TILE_SIZE; jj++) {
```

```
                              // Load B into SIMD register
                              b_tile = _mm512_load_ps(&B[kk][jj]);

                              // Compute C = A * B
                              c_tile = _mm512_fmadd_ps(a_tile, b_tile,
    _mm512_load_ps(&C[ii][jj]));

                              // Store C back
                              _mm512_store_ps(&C[ii][jj], c_tile);
                          }
                      }
                  }
              }
          }
    }
```

x86 Assembly Instructions used in GEMM in CPU:

Feature	FP32 GEMM	INT8 GEMM (Without VNNI)	INT8 GEMM (With VNNI)
Multiply-Add	VFMADD231PS (FMA)	VPMADDUBSW + VPMADDWD + VPADDD	VPDPBUSD or VPDPBUSDS
Accumulation	FP32 (zmm registers)	INT32 (VPADDD) or INT16 (**VPMADDUBSW**)	INT32 (VPDPBUSD)
Memory Loads	VMOVUPS, VBROADCASTSS	VPBROADCASTB, VPBROADCASTD	VPBROADCASTB, VPBROADCASTD
Efficiency	Compute-bound, high precision	Memory-bound, requires explicit accumulation	Optimized, reduces instruction count by 3X

Instruction Count per Dot-Product	1 (VFMADD231PS)	3 (VPMADDUBSW + VPMADDWD + VPADDD)	1 (VPDPBUSD)
Performance Impact	Higher precision, slower than INT8	Higher latency due to extra instructions	3X faster than non-VNNI INT8 GEMM

To understand assembly instruction, example:

VPDPBUSD takes 4 pairs of signed bytes (4 INT8) and corresponding unsigned bytes (4 UINT8) and does the dot product and saves the sum in xmm1 register. This instruction is available only in AVX-VNNI instruction set architecture.

Similarly, for INT8 GEMM (without VNNI), **VPMADDUBSW** takes 2 pairs of INT8 numbers, does the dot product and saves the result in INT16 (no sum). **VPMADDWD** sums the 2 INT16 numbers as INT32 result and **VPADDD** accumulates the INT32 result.

So, the VNNI version of INT8 GEMM takes 1 instruction which takes 4 pairs of input and takes 2 clock cycles for execution.

For non-VNNI version of INT8 GEMM, 3 instructions are involved taking 2 pairs of input and 1 clock cycle for each instruction (3 in total).

So, **VNNI INT8 GEMM is 3X faster.**

Convolution operation [1989]

Convolution and Attention are two basic operations that have revolutionized DL.

Convolution is an operation that has two inputs:

- Input image of size NxM
- Input kernel of size KxK

Usually, K << N or M. In real models, K is 1, 3, 5, 7 or 11.

The operation involves the dot-product of the kernel with every possible sub-matrix of same size KxK of input image. The answer of the dot-product is the output at the same index as the top left element of the sub-matrix of input image.

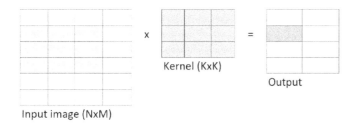

Kernel (KxK)

Output

Input image (NxM)

Convolution can be implemented using GEMM after transforming the input to a custom format using **im2row / im2col** (image to column).

There are other techniques like kn2row.

For an image of size N^2 and kernel of size K^2, the time complexity of Convolution is **$O(N^2 K^2)$**.

Convolution operation take up **70% of the inference time for CNN models**.

Intuitively, Convolution is used to extract/highlight specific features from the input image. The features extracted depend on the weights (kernel).

The weight values are determined during training.

Variants of Convolution implementations:

Method	Description	Advantages	Disadvantages	Use Cases
Direct Convolution	Standard approach, performs element-wise MACs directly on the input feature map.	No preprocessing overhead, simple to implement.	Slow for large kernels, poor memory reuse.	Small kernels (e.g., 3×3), hardware accelerators with optimized support.
GEMM-based Convolution (im2row/im2col)	Converts input tensor to a 2D matrix (im2row) and performs matrix multiplication.	Leverages optimized GEMM libraries, maximizes data reuse.	Im2row transformation adds overhead, high memory consumption.	Large CNNs, when highly optimized GEMM is available.
JIT-based Convolution	Generates highly optimized machine code at runtime based on hardware capabilities.	Maximized hardware utilization, fine-grained optimizations.	Higher initial compilation time, complex implementation.	Performance-critical deep learning workloads.

Depthwise Separable Convolution	Splits convolution into depthwise (per-channel) and pointwise (1×1) convolutions.	Reduces computational complexity, improves efficiency.	Not as effective for small models, requires framework support.	MobileNet, low-power AI inference.
Grouped Convolution	Splits channels into groups and performs independent convolutions.	Reduces parameter count, enables efficient training.	Limited flexibility, requires framework support.	Efficient training, ResNeXt-style architectures.
1x1 Convolution (Pointwise Convolution)	Uses a 1×1 kernel to mix channels.	Extremely efficient, enables feature reduction and channel mixing.	Not directly useful for spatial filtering.	Bottleneck layers in deep CNNs (e.g., MobileNet, ResNet).
Sparse Convolution	Skips zero or redundant elements in input to save computation.	Efficient for sparse inputs, reduces computation.	Requires specialized hardware or libraries.	3D point cloud processing (e.g., sparse CNNs in LIDAR applications).

Some core optimization techniques for Convolution:

Optimization	Purpose & Explanation

Tiling (16×K Blocking, Cache Blocking)	Improves cache locality by processing smaller tiles of data, reducing cache thrashing and memory bandwidth bottlenecks. Common sizes: 16×K, 32×K for efficient L1/L2 utilization.
Prefetching & Software Pipelining	Hides memory latency by preloading data into cache before it is needed, overlapping memory loads with computation. Utilizes intrinsics like _mm_prefetch.
Vectorized Computation (SIMD, VNNI, AVX512, Tensor Cores)	Uses hardware acceleration (SIMD/VNNI on CPU, Tensor Cores on GPU) for parallel processing. INT8 computations leverage VNNI (VPDPBUSD) or AVX512 (VPMADDUBSW + VPMADDWD). FP32 uses VFMADD231PS for fused multiply-add.
Using INT16 Accumulation Instead of INT32 for INT8 Convolution	Reduces register pressure and memory bandwidth for INT8 GEMM. Uses VPMADDUBSW + VPADDW instead of INT32 VPDPBUSD, leading to a 1.5-2X speedup in some cases. Useful for AMD Zen3/Zen4 CPUs without AVX512 VNNI.
Weight Reordering (NHWC to NCHW, Blocked Format)	Reorders weights to match optimal memory access patterns. Blocked format (e.g., 16×K) ensures efficient vectorized loads. Common transformations include NHWC → NCHW16c for AVX512 and NCHW → NC/4HW4 for GPU execution.
Weight Input Cached (as it Remains Same)	In inference workloads, weights do not change, so they can be preloaded into faster memory (L2/L3 cache or SRAM in accelerators) to minimize DRAM access.
Post-op Fusion (ReLU, BatchNorm in Kernel)	Reduces memory bandwidth overhead by fusing elementwise operations (ReLU, BatchNorm, Bias Add) directly within the convolution kernel. Reduces redundant memory accesses.

JIT-based Optimization	Generates highly optimized machine code at runtime based on hardware features (e.g., AVX512, VNNI, AMX). Utilizes frameworks like Xbyak for x86, CUDA PTX for NVIDIA GPUs, and MLIR for LLVM-based optimizations.
kn2row for GEMM Convolution	Alternative to im2row for better memory efficiency. Converts input tensors into a form that aligns well with cache-line access patterns, avoiding redundant memory loads. Works well for small kernel sizes (e.g., 3×3).
Efficient Memory Layout for Tensor Cores (GPU)	NVIDIA Tensor Cores require specific memory layouts (e.g., FP16 WMMA 16×16×16). Optimized memory alignment ensures minimal bank conflicts and maximized throughput.

Deep Learning System Design

Understanding different components in DL pipeline to create an application open up deep practical insights. Do not learn just theory and optimizations. Use it.

Steps in approaching a DL system design problem (*use keywords*):

- **Step 0:** Understand the problem. *Make your own reasonable assumptions and estimate usage volume.*
- **Step 1**: Classify the problem as **recall-heavy** or **precision-heavy** or **recall-precision-balanced**.
- **Step 2**: Define sources of training data and features to be used. Address class imbalance. Define **supervised or unsupervised** learning. For supervised data preparation, form *labelling team*. Normalize, augment dataset. Remove outlier.
- **Step 3**: Define the models (may be **multi-stage, multi-tower, ensemble** + CNN, RNN, BERT, T5, multi-modal LLM + simple models like Regression, K-Means Clustering, Rule-based). Finetune pre-trained models.
- **Step 4**: Define training strategy, dataset split (train, validation, test), loss functions (**F1, F0.5, F2, Focal loss**), Regularization (dropout, L2), Optimizer (Adam, SGD)
- **Step 5**: Human feedback loop, Moderation team? Regular finetuning and calibration. Define evaluation (accuracy, precision, ROC-AUC, F1-score). Cross validation to test generalization. Bias prevention (SHAP, LIME).
- **Step 6**: Model deployment. Use Federated learning (Finetune on user device, use LoRA). Use **INT8/FP8 quantization, pruning, model distillation**. Use server (AI inference chip like **Intel Gaudi**) or edge devices.

Basic concepts:

If system is **recall heavy**:

- High recall -> **less false negative** (detect NSFW, disease, ...)
- **More caution**; Let moderation and secondary filter to handle false positive.

- Adjust **classification threshold**: lower decision threshold from 0.5 to 0.3, ensure more cases are classified as positive.
- Use **ensemble of high precision and high recall models**. Combine text-based, image-based, and user-feedback models. Use voting mechanism.
- **Multi-Stage Filtering**: 1st high-recall model (with false positive) (simple like keyword matching) -> 2nd precision-focused model to reduce false positive (transformer based)
- **Increase Coverage with More Features**: Use device type, past transactions, geolocation, image, text and user feedback together.
- Use **Human Review**: retraining
- Use **Recall-Optimized Loss Function**: Focal Loss, Recall-Weighted Loss. Do not use cross entropy.
- Consider **recall in model metrics**: Recall in topK, F2 score, ROC curve, AUC (select operating point with high recall)

If system is **precision heavy**:

- High precision -> **less false positive**
- Example: spam email filter, object detection in car
- Increase decision threshold.
- Use highly specific features like "contain links" vs "number of external links per word".
- Multi-stage filtering: Stage 1 (fast model with low threshold), Stage 2 (expensive more accurate model), Stage 3 (optional, human review/rule-based system)
    - Example: spam filter: Stage 1 (flag email with "urgent" or "win money"), Stage 2 (BERT for email context), Stage 3 (if model confidence is low, go for human review)
- Loss function: Focal loss (focus on confident prediction), Weighted loss, Precision weighted Hinge Loss
- Model Calibration: temperature scaling (lower confidence probability for prediction)
- Use F0.5 score; ROC and PR curve prioritizing precision

If system is recall-precision balanced:

- Both false positive and false negative is costly.
- Example: face recognition system for entry.
- Handle class imbalance; Use k-fold cross validation for generalization.
- Use F1 score (harmonic mean between recall and precision).
- Loss function: Use cross entropy

System to classify tweets as toxic or non-toxic

Core points:

We have a labeled data marking tweets (texts) as toxic (0) or non-toxic (1).

- **Data preprocessing**
  - Byte Pair Encoding (BPE) based tokenization.
  - Handle class imbalance by generating synthetic toxic tweets by **back translation** (Eng -> Hindi -> Eng) + **Paraphrase augmentation** (use alternate words) (**T5 model**)
  - Use Focal Loss instead of Cross Entropy (to put focus on less dense class)
- Use a **Transformer-based baseline model** (RoBERTa/DeBERTa) + Full Connected Layer (FC) + Softmax (for one label per input) / Sigmoid (for multi-labels per input)
  - RoBERTa is a **transformer-based encoder-only model**
  - Good contextual understanding, handling sarcasm & ambiguity better. No classifier head and low throughput for GPT4/Llama.
  - Already trained on language. **Finetune on toxic tweet dataset.**
  - Contrastive Learning to make it robust. SimCSE
  - Multi-task learning (+ emotion detection)
  - Adversarial Training (make error in words hate -> h8te)
- **Training**
  - Model is pretrained. Finetune on toxic tweet dataset.
  - Focal Loss (solves class imbalance), Label Smoothing (reduces overconfidence)

- Optimizer: AdamW (with weight decay), Learning Rate Scheduler: Cosine Annealing
  - Dropout layer + Layer Normalization to prevent overfitting
- **Deployment + Inference**
  - Convert to TinyBERT / DistilBERT / DistilRoBERTa using transfer learning.
  - Use INT8 quantization + Pruning.
  - Use TensorRT for GPU acceleration, Use TFLite for edge inference
- **Evaluation**
  - Metrics: Precision + Recall + F1 score (to check focus on toxic class), Area under ROC curve (for imbalanced data), False Positive Rate (for fairness)
  - Bias prevention: SHAP: SHapley Additive exPlanations: Compute contribution of each word to final prediction + LIME (Local Interpretable Model-Agnostic Explanations) change one word and see if output changes.
- **Feedback loop**
  - Human monitoring for false positives/negatives.
  - Active learning: Model queries users for harder cases
  - Federated learning: Finetune on user device without uploading user data on central server. LoRA (Low-Rank Adaptation) → Fine-tune only small adapter layers, Sparse updates -> send only important model weights.

Above model can be seen as a ground truth model. A tweet can be toxic for one user but not for another. **To include user preference**:

- **Tweet Tower**: (Above trained DistilRoBERTa to get a tweet embedding, skip fusion layer).
- **User Tower**:
  - Static attributes: age, location, language, ...
  - Dynamic attributes: Number of reports/blocks (more sensitive), ...
  - Identify bias/sensitivity to topics:
    - Use Named Entity Recognition NER (using **BERT based NER**) to detect **entities** (like celebrities).

- Use **BERTopic** to detect **abstract topics** (ideology). Uses unsupervised learning.
- Based on user interaction, create affinity vector for each entity and abstract topic. Use simple MLP.
- Create user embedding (take topK of entities/abstract topics)
- Fuse tweet embedding + user embedding (simple concatenation or attention-based fusion). Can be done on user device.
- Use Fusion layer (FC + Sigmoid) for final personalized toxic tweet detection.

If you want to **include reports by users into the process**:

- Create embedding for each user. Create cluster of users based on common toxicity reports (using K-Means or GNN community detection)
- Create cluster of toxic tweets using BERT + Clustering.
- Train both models as multi-modal model such that the user embedding and toxic tweet embedding is aligned.
- For a new user, find the topK closest user group. For each user group, find TopM toxic tweet abstract topics. For these M*K tweet embeddings, find the similarity of the current tweet.

Design an evaluation framework for ads ranking

There is an existing ad ranking system in Instagram. A team has created a new ad ranking system but A/B testing on real time is expensive.

Create a DL system to evaluate this new ad ranking system locally.

1. Problem

Input:

- **Ranking of N ads** = The ordered list of ads for a user.
- **User ID** = Helps retrieve historic data for personalization.

Output:

- **CTR Prediction** = Probability of clicking on each of the N ads.

24

- **Time Spent Prediction** = Estimated time spent viewing each ad.
- **Revenue impact** for Instagram + Client

2. Key Features for Evaluation

To predict CTR and Time Spent, we need embeddings from different sources:

(a) Ad Feature Representation

Each ad has text + image + metadata (like category, brand).

- CNN extracts deep visual features from ad images.
- RoBERTa encodes textual descriptions.
- Metadata is converted to embeddings via MLP.

Final Ad Embedding: Fused from CNN (image), Transformer (text), and MLP (metadata) = 512D embedding

(b) Historic User Data Embedding

Already available in user database:

- Past interaction history (clicks, skips, likes).
- Topics of interest (modeled via **BERTopic**).
- Preferred ad engagement patterns (image ads, video ads).

Final User Embedding: Learned using a BERT (Transformer) (long sequential data) encodes past behavior into a dense vector.

(c) Current Context Embedding

Can be real data or stimulated context. Includes:

- Time of day (morning vs night impacts engagement).
- Device Type (mobile vs desktop).
- User Mood (estimated via recent interactions).

Can be encoded using:

- Learned embedding lookup for categorical feature ["iphone"] -> [0.3, 0.2]
- MLP for contiguous features
  - MLP([Session Length = 10 min, Battery Level = 40%]) → [0.1, 0.9, -0.2]

Final Context Embedding: MLP encoding of all real-time context factors.

(d) Current Feed Embedding

User's feed before and after seeing the ads affects their mood.

We take:

- M previous posts + interactions (likes, comments, skips).
- M next posts + expected engagement.

Final Feed Embedding: Uses a Transformer-based sequence model (BERT/GPT) to encode past and future posts.

Captures user attention drift (e.g., user moves from serious news → casual ads).

3. Fusion of All Embeddings

We now have:

- Ad Embedding (CNN + Transformer + Metadata MLP).
- User Embedding (Historic Behavior from Transformer/RNN).
- Context Embedding (MLP encoding of real-time features).
- Feed Embedding (Transformer-based sequence model).

Fusion Strategy

- Option 1 (Concatenation + FC Layer): Simple and effective.

Just concatenate all embeddings into a single 2048D representation and pass it through a Fully Connected (FC) layer with non-linearity (ReLU).

- Option 2 (Cross-Attention): Instead of simple concatenation, we use a Transformer cross-attention layer where:
  - The Ad embedding is the query.

- o The User and Context embeddings are the keys and values.
- o This allows dynamic weighting based on real-time context.

Final Combined Embedding: A 2048D fused vector representing the relationship between the ad, user, feed and context.

4. Prediction Layer (CTR and Time Spent)

Now that we have the fused embedding, we predict CTR and Time Spent.

- **CTR Prediction**: Softmax over {Click, No Click}
- **Time Spent Prediction**: ReLU (so no negative value) + Regression Head (FC): time in seconds
- **Revenue impact**: Conversion rate for client + Direct revenue calculation for Instagram from predicted CTR

5. Synthetic validation dataset

Generate synthetic validation data for:

- Feed of M previous posts
- Current session context (time, device)

Approaches:

- **Use existing feed ranking system**: Pass synthetic posts and get ranking
- Random Sampling from a Defined Set of categories
- Use LLM like GPT4 for realistic feed data or synthetic posts.

6. Explainability using SHAP and LIME

SHAP (Shapley Additive Explanations):

- Used to understand which features impact CTR most.
- For instance, SHAP might reveal that "Brand Loyalty" is the dominant factor for a particular user segment.

LIME (Local Interpretable Model-agnostic Explanations):

- Used to interpret individual predictions.
- Example: Why did the model predict high time spent on an ad?
- LIME shows that past engagement with similar ads and current content on feed contributed highly.

6. Feedback Loop

The new ranking system is updated based on this evaluation.

Personalized news ranking system

Step 1: Problem Definition

Objective: Rank news articles dynamically for each user based on:

- User Interests (past interactions, explicit preferences, implicit behaviors)
- News Article Relevance (freshness, credibility, topic, context)
- Engagement Likelihood (CTR, dwell time, shares, comments)
- Bias Control (avoid echo chambers, ensure diversity)
- Real-Time Adaptation (trending events, breaking news)

Step 2: Data Collection & Processing

User Data: Past interactions (clicked, shared, read time), explicit preferences
        User Embedding via Transformers/RNN

News Article Features Headline, body, category, publisher, sentiment   BERT-based encoding

Temporal Context embeddings	Trending topics, real-time news updates	Time-aware
Device & Session Embeddings	Mobile/Desktop, session duration	Categorical

Step 3: Model Architecture

A Hybrid Two-Tower Deep Learning Model with Contrastive Learning for personalization.

User Tower (Encodes User Preferences)

- Static user data: location, language, age, explicit interests [embedding]
- Transformer-based model (BERT / DistilBERT / LLaMA) encodes past N interactions. Augment with
    - Topic Modeling (BERTopic)
    - (News writer, celebrity) Entity Modeling (BERT NER).
- Capture user affinity towards topics, entities & publishers.
- Capture both long term and short-term interests.
    - BERT on entire history or last N articles (N >> M): Long term interests
    - LSTM on recent M articles: short term interests
    - **User embedding = α * short-term + (1 – α) * long-term**
    - Or just use time-based BERT: Final User Embedding = **Weighted Sum (Historical Interactions + Recency Boost)**
- Convert categorical features (device, time of day) into temporal embedding.
- Output: Dense 512D user embedding.

News Tower (Encodes News Articles)

- BERT-based encoder for headline, body for all news: [news database]
- Select Top 10,000 news: **FAISS**: Nearest Neighbor search on vector space of news.
    - Use time decay for old news.

29

- o **Query**: User embedding: static topics/interests + recent interests.
- Additional metadata: Publisher, category, sentiment = MLP encoder
- Temporal context encoding via RNN / Transformer for evolving trends.
- Output: Dense 512D news embedding for K news each

Fusion Layer

- Combines user embedding + news embedding + temporal context
- Cross-attention mechanism to highlight relevant features
- Output: Final fused representation

Multi-task learning:

- **Ranking Head** (FC + Softmax for News Scores + Sort). Final ranking:
    - o System gives ranking for N articles.
    - o Multi-Armed Bandits for Exploration-Exploitation: UCB/Thompson Sampling decide whether to show higher ranked article or new unexplored article.
- **CTR Prediction** (FC + Softmax)
- **Dwell Time Regression** (FC + ReLU)

Step 4: Training & Optimization

- **Contrastive Learning (SimCSE)** to improve user-news matching: ensure similar news/user interactions have closer embeddings while dissimilar ones are pushed apart
- **Pairwise Ranking Loss (Triplet Loss)**: Encourages correct ranking order by considering clicked news, skipped news, user embedding.
- **Focal Loss** for handling skewed user engagement: weights down easy skipped news, focus on harder misclassified samples.
- **Adversarial Training (FGSM)** (Fast Gradient Sign Method) to improve generalization: small perturbations added to input during training to make model robust.

Step 5: Inference & Real-Time Serving

- Re-Ranking Model (Transformer-based) for final ranking
- Feedback loop via SHAP/LIME to detect bias
    - **SHAP** (Shapley Additive Explanations): Impact of each feature on ranking
    - **LIME** (Local Interpretable Model-Agnostic Explanations): Generates perturbed news samples and checks impact on ranking.
- If **bias is detected**:
    - Adjust feature weights, re-rank with diversity constraints, remove bias from embedding, fix FAISS +diversity aware retrieval, RL to award engagement and diversity, UCB/Thompson sampling to balance exploration + exploitation.
- **RL feedback loop**
    - **Agent** = ranking model
    - **Environment**: real world user interactions
    - **Actions**: ranking
    - **Reward**: engagement with diverse content, diversity bonus to prevent filter bubble
    - **Policy update**: ranking model parameters updated based on reward, UCB/Thompson sampling to balance exploration/exploitation

Step 6: Evaluation & Feedback

- CTR Uplift: Measures engagement improvement
- Dwell Time Increase: Longer reads indicate better ranking
- Diversity Score: Ensures varied news sources & topics
- Cold Start User Performance: Measures effectiveness for new users

Product Recommendation

Given a stock of products in Amazon, create a ranking of recommended products for a given user.

Data pipeline

Data Type	Examples	Processing & Storage
User Data	Clicks, views, cart, purchases, ratings, dwell time	Stored in **real-time event streaming** (Kafka, Flink)
Product Data	Categories, images, price, descriptions	Stored in **vector DB (FAISS, Milvus)**
Context Data	Device, location, time, weather, browsing history	Processed using **feature engineering pipeline**
External Signals	Trending products, social signals, influencer trends	NLP-based **topic modeling (BERTopic, LDA)**

Candidate products

Quickly keyword to retrieve Top-K (~10,000) relevant products from millions. Methods:

- Sparse Retrieval (BM25, TF-IDF): Fast text-based filtering.
- Dense Retrieval (**FAISS**, HNSW, Annoy): Nearest Neighbor Search (Embeddings).
- Graph-based Retrieval: Node2Vec over user-product graph for cold start.

There are 4 towers:

- User tower
- Product tower
- Business tower
- Trending product tower

User Tower (User Embedding)

Encodes user preferences, purchase history, and demographic features.

Model: Transformer or LSTM to capture long-term & short-term trends.

Input Features:

- Past interactions (clicks, purchases, cart add, dwell time).
- Demographics (age, location, device type).

- Temporal features (seasonality, time of day).

Output: 512D User Embedding

Product Tower (Product Embedding)

Model:

- BERT (for textual metadata: product description, category)
- ResNet / EfficientNet (for image-based features).
- Or Use a Multi-modal model like CLIP
- + **MLP** (for structured data like price, ratings).

Input Features: Title, description, Product image, Category, price, stock availability.

Output: 512D Product Embedding

Business Tower (Business Embedding)

Encodes business constraints such as profit margin, sponsored ranking boost, stock availability, and discounts.

Model: MLP or Embedding Table.

Input Features:

- **Profit Margin Score**: Higher margin products get boosted.
- **Sponsored Score**: Paid promotions.
- **Inventory Levels**: Low-stock products might be deprioritized.
- **Diversity Constraints**: Avoids recommending similar products.

Output: 128D Business Embedding

Trending product tower

Monitor external sources to identify emerging trends:

- **Social media**: Use **LLM** (LLaMA, GPT-4, DeepSeek) for Named Entity Recognition (NER) on captions/comments. **BERT-based NER** to extract brand names, product names, keywords. Hashtag and trend analysis using **TF-IDF or Topic Modeling (BERTopic, LDA)**.
- **News & Blogs**: Use Google News API or web crawlers to fetch articles. Run **BERT NER** to extract product mentions. Assign sentiment scores (Sentiment Analysis with **RoBERTa**).
- **TV Shows, Movies, Influencers**: Track show/movie metadata using OCR (on posters) + Speech Recognition (Whisper, Wav2Vec2). Use **BERT-based semantic matching to map detected items to product catalog**.
- **Search Trends (Google Trends, E-commerce Searches)**: Use **time-series forecasting models (LSTM, Prophet)** to detect rising search interest. Compare product searches on e-commerce vs external search trends.

Creating the External Trend Embedding (ETE)

Once trending products are identified, they are encoded into a new embedding space. Input to ETE Model:

- Product Name + Category (from catalog)
- Trend Strength (from social media, news, search)
- Sentiment Score (positive, negative, neutral)
- Time Decay Factor (Recency importance = older trends get lower weight)

Model:

- MLP-based embedding lookup: Converts categorical + numerical features into 128D embedding.
- Transformer or LSTM: To model time-series influence of trends.

Output:

- 128D External Trend Embedding (ETE)

Fusion

All 4 embeddings are fused. Attention-weighted fusion where higher trend strength = higher weight.

- Takes combined 1152D vector and passes through FC layers.
- Uses ReLU activations for non-linearity.

Multi-task learning:

- Outputs a final ranking score.
- Product buying prediction score.
- Reviewing a product prediction.

To prevent excessive bias towards trending products:

- Decay Over Time: Trends fade exponentially (use time-aware embeddings).
- Personalization Check: Ensure trending products align with user preferences.
- Business Constraints: If trends conflict with business goals, adjust ranking.

Understand FC + Concatenation

If user embedding is 512D, product embedding is 512D and then is 10,000 candidate products:

(10K, 512D) + (512D) = (10K, 1024D)

Layer	Input Shape	Output Shape	Activation
FC1	(10,000, 1024)	(10,000, 512)	ReLU
FC2	(10,000, 512)	(10,000, 128)	ReLU
FC3 (Final)	(10,000, 128)	(10,000, 1)	No Activation (Raw Score)

Inference & Real-Time Serving

- Ranking Model (Transformer-based) for final ranking
- Feedback loop via SHAP/LIME to detect bias

- o **SHAP** (Shapley Additive Explanations): Impact of each feature on ranking
- o **LIME** (Local Interpretable Model-Agnostic Explanations): Generates perturbed news samples and checks impact on ranking.
- If **bias is detected**:
  - o Adjust feature weights, re-rank with diversity constraints, remove bias from embedding, fix FAISS +diversity aware retrieval, RL to award engagement and diversity, UCB/Thompson sampling to balance exploration + exploitation.
- **RL feedback loop**
  - o **Agent** = ranking model
  - o **Environment**: real world user interactions
  - o **Actions**: ranking
  - o **Reward**: product purchase
  - o **Policy update**: ranking model parameters updated based on reward, UCB/Thompson sampling to balance exploration/exploitation

If model underperforms?

- Data drift = Use contrastive learning to detect changes.
- Model overfitting = Use adversarial training.
- Bias detected via SHAP/LIME = Adjust loss function with fairness constraints.

Detect if image and description map to same product

- Use **ResNet50 or ViT (Vision Transformer)** pre-trained on image dataset; Fine-tune on product images; Get fixed-length embedding for product image
- Use **RoBERTa NER or T5** (pre-trained + fine-tuned on product descriptions); Convert description into embedding
- Align image and text embedding using **CLIP (Contrastive Language Image Pre-training)**

- Measure similarity: cosine similarity; If below a threshold, there is a mismatch. Notify user to update image/text.
  - Human monitoring for false positives/negatives on random flags.
  - Use higher precision model for user reports.
- Use contrastive loss (SimCLR) to improve embedding quality.

This can be used as components in detecting illegal items in a product listing.

INT8 Quantization

Understanding how to do calculations in INT8 instead of FP32 and still get same results is a core optimization in DL. DL is highly insensitive to local errors.

INT8 Quantization is a technique to run DL models by computing arithmetic using INT8 inputs (instead of FP32) with INT8 outputs. This reduces the memory bandwidth by 4X and improves computation by up to 3X (using AVX512 VNNI instructions).

For AVX details, see chapter on "**Matrix Multiplication**" and "**Convolution**".

By default, weights are in FP32 and computation is in FP32 as well. These are converted to INT8. The new pre-training model is a quantized INT8 model.

There are **3 basic approaches** to Quantization (preparing INT8 model):

Method	Description	Notes
Post-Training Quantization (PTQ)	Converts FP32 model to INT8 after training	Less accuracy, Fast training
Quantization-Aware Training (QAT)	Simulates INT8 during training for better accuracy	Higher accuracy, Full training needed
Dynamic Quantization	Only weights are INT8, activations remain FP32	Less benefit of INT8 speedup

Core concepts:

- FP32 input mapped to INT8 range
- Core operations: quantize, dequantize, clip
- Symmetric Quantization
- Asymmetric Quantization

FP32 input is mapped to INT8 range

Note: The distribution of numbers remains the same. Numbers can fall out of the INT8 range after conversion is clipped to the max or min INT8 value.

This involves 2 core metrics:

- Scale factor **S**
- Zero-point **Z**

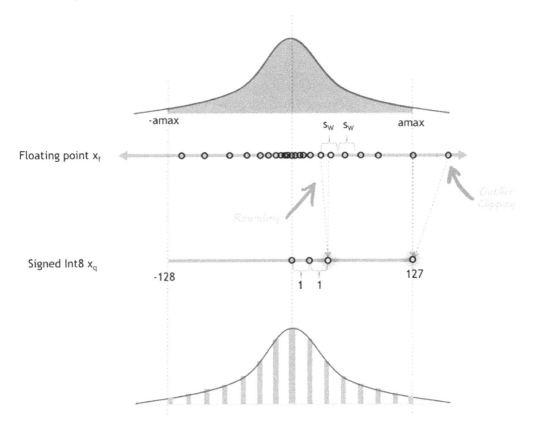

Quant/ Dequant operations

2 core operations using S and Z (X is input):

- Quantize operation: Convert FP32/INT32 inputs to INT8: X_q = **round(X/S + Z)**
    - **Output is clipped to fit in INT8 range [-128, 127] or [0, 255]**
- Dequantize operation: Convert INT8 to FP32/INT32: X_d = $(X_q - Z)$ * **S**
    - **Output is clipped to the actual min / max of the input**

- Actual min / max is maintained through the model.

Op Type	Description	Used For
Quantize Per-Tensor	A single scale and zero-point are shared across all elements in the tensor.	Simple quantization when data distribution is uniform across the tensor.
Dequantize Per-Tensor	Dequantizes the entire tensor using a global scale and zero-point.	Complementary to Quantize Per-Tensor.
Quantize Per-Channel	Each channel in the tensor gets its own scale and zero-point, allowing finer control.	Quantizing tensors with varying channel distributions (e.g., CNN weights).
Dequantize Per-Channel	Dequantizes each channel using a unique scale and zero-point.	Complementary to Quantize Per-Channel.
Quantize Per-Block	Quantization applied on a block of the tensor, often used when processing large batches or operations.	Used in optimizations like block-level quantization to manage large tensor blocks.
Dequantize Per-Block	Dequantizes each block using a unique scale and zero-point, similar to per-channel but at a block level.	Complementary to Quantize Per-Block.
Clip	Clips the input values to be within a specified range (e.g., [-128, 127] for INT8).	Ensures that values are within the representable range for INT8.

S and Z is computed as:

Symmetric Quantization

If input has range [X_{min}, X_{max}] where the middle element is 0, then:

$$\text{Scale} = \frac{MAX\ (|X_{min}|,\ |X_{max}|)}{2^{N-1}-1}$$

Zero point = 0 (always)

Main points:

- INT8 range is **[-127, 127]** (Input is mapped to this range)
- Use when input data is centered around zero (not + or – skewed)
- Efficient computation as zero-point addition is avoided.
- In relative symmetric input, gives better accuracy as it captures small values better (example, weights in CNN)

Asymmetric Quantization

$$S = \frac{X_{MAX} - X_{MIN}}{2^N - 1}$$

$$Z = ROUND(\frac{-Xmin}{S})$$

Main points:

- INT8 range is **[-128, 127]** (if signed output is needed) or **[0, 255]**
- Captures full dynamic range of input.
- Better accuracy for highly skewed input (ReLU output)

Feature	Symmetric Quantization	Asymmetric Quantization
INT8 range	[-127, 127]	[0, 255] or [-128, 127]
Zero-point (Z)	Always 0	Computed (Z ≠ 0)
Use case	Balanced distributions	Skewed distributions
Compute efficiency	Faster	Extra computation (addition of zero point)
Accuracy	Better for symmetric input	Better for skewed input

There are 2 main methods of preparing an INT8 model:

- PTQ
- QAT

Post Training Quantization (PTQ)

Main steps:

- Take a pre-trained FP32 model.

- For **weights**, calculate the range and compute the scale and zero point accordingly using symmetric quantization.
- For **activations**, run inference on a subset of the training dataset (called calibration dataset) and measure the range of activations. Clip the outliers using **histogram-based calibration** and compute the scale and zero point according using asymmetric quantization. This step is called **calibration**.
- Run inference using the computed scale and zero point.
    - If accuracy is low, update the calibration step.
    - As PTQ is sensitive, **first Conv layer must run in FP32** and specific ops like SoftMax should run in FP32. Fuse specific ops like Conv + BatchNorm + ReLU.
- If accuracy remains low, **QAT** must be used.

Quantization-Aware Training (QAT)

Main steps:

- Take the **FP32 model**.
- Before each op which needs to be quantized (like Conv), add a Fake Quantization op (that is Quantize -> Dequantize one after another). This **introduces INT8 quantization noise in training process**.
- In **forward pass**, ops like Conv run in the default FP32 precision.
- In **backward pass**, the loss gradient is bypassed through the Fake Quantization. This is called **straight-through estimator STE**. Weights are updated as usual.
- At the end of the training process, the Fake Quantization nodes hold the scale and zero point.

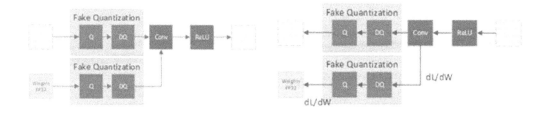

Calibration

- Process: clip original weights -> then quantization (avoid outlier + increase representation) -> improves accuracy.
- Manually choose percentile of weights to consider.
- Minimize mean squared error (MSE) between **original and quantized weight**.
- Minimizing entropy (KL-divergence) between **original and quantized value**.

GPU Workload Parallelization

Understanding how to run a workload on GPU in parallel is an important skill of a Deep Learning Engineer. **Make full use of the hardware.**

GPU architecture

A GPU architecture can be viewed as follows:

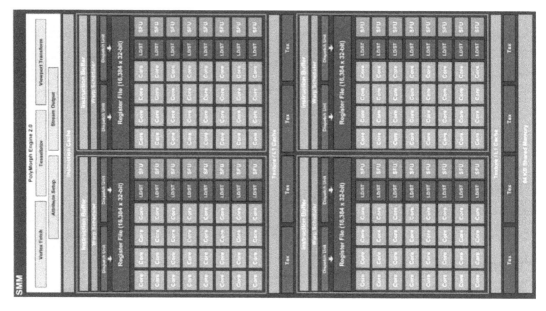

Note: there are 4 distinct parts. Each part is called a **wrap**.

A wrap has 8x4 = **32 cores** which run in **SIMT** mode. No explicit synchronization is needed at wrap level (in **lockstep**).

The complete setup is called a block = 4 wraps = 4x32 = 128 cores. At block level, threads from different wraps need to be synchronized (reduction).

A complete GPU chip may have up to 16 blocks = 16x128 = 2048 cores.

A single thread can run on a single core.

Parallel Execution Strategies (general concepts)

44

Work Distribution

- **Data Parallelism**: Apply the same computation to different parts of data. Split data into smaller data.
- **Task Parallelism**: Different threads perform different tasks. Split task into smaller independent tasks.
- **Hybrid Parallelism**: Mix data and task parallelism for efficiency.

Run algorithms in parallel

- **Domain Decomposition**: Split problem into smaller independent subproblems. Example: Tile based MatMul.
- **Recursive Parallelism**: Used in divide-and-conquer algorithms (e.g., QuickSort, MergeSort).
- **Reduction and Scan**: Efficient prefix sum, min/max operations, and histogram generation.

Load Balancing

- **Static Scheduling**: Predefined workload per thread.
- **Dynamic Scheduling**: Work is distributed dynamically based on demand.
- **Work Stealing**: Threads dynamically take work from others when idle.

Optimizing Parallel Performance

Memory Optimization

- **Coalesced Memory Access in a wrap**: Threads in a warp should access consecutive memory addresses.
- **Shared Memory Usage**: Store frequently accessed data in shared memory (avoid bank conflicts).
- **Register Usage**: Minimize spilling into local memory.

Concept	Explanation
Register Spill	Happens when a kernel uses too many registers per thread.

Where does it go?	Spill happens in **local memory (which maps to global memory, DRAM)**, not shared memory.
Why not Shared Memory?	Shared memory is managed **explicitly** by the programmer, not automatically by the compiler.
Fix?	Reduce register usage Use less variables Use shared memory for temporary storage like array.

Code which creates an array of 128 integers for each thread. This increases the register use and causes register spill.

```cpp
// SYCL code with register spill
#include <CL/sycl.hpp>
using namespace sycl;

int main() {
    queue q;
    constexpr int N = 1024;
    buffer<int, 1> buf(N);

    q.submit([&](handler& h) {
        accessor acc(buf, h, read_write);
        h.parallel_for(nd_range<1>{N, 256}, [=](nd_item<1> item) {
            int idx = item.get_global_id(0);
            // High register pressure (potential spill)
            int large_array[128];

            // Initialize array
            for (int i = 0; i < 128; i++) {
                large_array[i] = idx + i;
            }

            // Compute sum (Reduction)
            int sum = 0;
            for (int i = 0; i < 128; i++) {
                sum += large_array[i];
            }

            // Store the result back
            acc[idx] = sum;
        });
```

```
        }).wait();
}
```

Fixed code using shared memory:

```cpp
// SYCL code without register spill
// Uses shared memory
#include <CL/sycl.hpp>
using namespace sycl;

int main() {
    sycl::queue q;
    constexpr int N = 1024;
    constexpr int BLOCK_SIZE = 256;

    sycl::buffer<int, 1> buf(N);

    q.submit([&](sycl::handler& h) {
        sycl::accessor acc(buf, h, sycl::read_write);

        // Each thread gets its own private space inside shared memory
        // 256 x 128 array
        sycl::local_accessor<int, 2>
sharedMem(sycl::range<2>(BLOCK_SIZE, 128), h);

        h.parallel_for(sycl::nd_range<1>{N, BLOCK_SIZE},
[=](sycl::nd_item<1> item)
        {
            int idx = item.get_global_id(0);
            int lid = item.get_local_id(0);

            // Each thread gets its own private memory inside shared
memory
            for (int j = 0; j < 128; j++) {
                sharedMem[lid][j] = idx + j;
            }

            // Ensure all threads finish before summing
            item.barrier();

            // Compute the sum for each thread's private shared memory
space
            int sum = 0;
            for (int j = 0; j < 128; j++) {
                sum += sharedMem[lid][j];
```

47

```
        }
        acc[idx] = sum;
    });
}).wait();
}
```

- **Memory Prefetching**: Load data before it is needed.

Reducing Thread Divergence

- **Avoid conditionals in Warps**: If-else conditions inside a warp can cause serialization.
- **Warp-Level Primitives**: Use shuffle, ballot, and warp reduce to optimize intra-warp communication.

Asynchronous Execution

- **Streams and Pipelines**: Overlap kernel execution and memory transfers.
- **Graph APIs**: Optimize execution flow by using command graphs in SYCL.

CPU vs GPU

CPU = optimized for low-latency, out-of-order execution with complex control logic

GPU = optimized for high throughput with massive parallelism

SIMD vs SIMT

Conce pts	SIMD	SIMT
#1	Single instruction is applied to multiple data elements in parallel.	Multiple threads execute the same instruction but with different data.
#2	Uses **vectorized operations (AVX/SSE)** which stores multiple data in a register and executes one	Threads are grouped into warps (32 threads per warp). **Each thread uses a vectorized instruction similar to SIMD**. Some

	instruction (like sum of 4 elements in one clock cycle).	GPUs do use SIMD for each thread in SIMT.
#3	Requires contiguous data and does not handle divergence well. AVX instructions are of fixed width like **SIMD16**.	If all threads in a warp follow the same execution path, they execute in **lockstep** (no explicit synchronization). If they diverge, execution becomes serialized.

Each thread has a private set of registers.

If too many registers are used, some will "spill" into local memory

GPU execution model is organized into different levels:

- **Thread (Work-item)**: Smallest unit of execution.
  - ○ In general, every output element is assigned a separate work-item.
  - ○ Ensure each thread access contiguous memory.
- **Warp (CUDA) / Wavefront (AMD)**: A group of 32 (CUDA) or 64 (AMD) threads executing in lockstep.
  - ○ Inter-wrap communication is efficient (reduction/shuffle).
  - ○ Avoid warp divergence: Avoid if else conditions
- **Block (CUDA) / Workgroup (SYCL)**: A collection of warps executing together, sharing memory.
  - ○ Tiling: Use shared memory to reduce global memory access.
- **Grid (CUDA) / ND-Range (SYCL)**: The entire execution space across all blocks.
  - ○ Optimal workgroup sizing: Ensure enough blocks to saturate GPU cores.
  - ○ Load balancing: Distribute workload evenly across the grid.

Special GPU operations:

- **Shuffle**

Allows threads within a warp (32 threads) to exchange data without shared/global memory.

Example of finding sum of all values across threads in a wrap:

- Thread i fetches data from i + offset.
- Reduces the number of active threads by half in each step.
- Only thread 0 has the complete sum.

```
float warpReduceSum(sub_group sg, float val) {
    for (int offset = sg.get_max_local_range()[0] / 2; offset > 0;
offset /= 2) {
        val += sg.shuffle_down(val, offset);
    }
    return val;
}
```

- **Broadcast**

Broadcasts a single value from one thread to all others in the same warp.

Example: Fetches val from thread 0 and distributes it to all warp threads.

```
float leaderValue = sg.shuffle(val, 0);
```

- **Reduction (wrap level or block level)**

Computes sum, min, max, product of values across a warp or block.

```
float warpReduce(sub_group sg, float val) {
    return reduce_over_group(sg, val, plus<float>());
}
```

- **Exclusive Scan & Inclusive Scan**

Exclusive scan computes the prefix sum excluding the current element (Inclusive includes the current element).

```
int scan(sub_group sg, int val) {
```

```
      return exclusive_scan_over_group(sg, val, plus<int>());
}
```

- **Ballot**

Returns a bitmask of which threads meet a condition; Used in warp-level parallel decisions.

Special GPU concepts

Efficiency measure:

- **GPU Occupancy**: Number of active threads in a block / Maximum number of threads in a block
- **Register usage per thread** (less is better)
- Number of **global memory access** (less is better)
- Balance between **block size and grid size**.

Warp Divergence: when threads in a wrap follow different paths due to if-else conditions. The execution gets serialized. Avoid conditions.

GPU memory hierarchy

- Register: 1X access time (exclusive to each thread)
- Shared memory: 10X access time (exclusive to each block)
- Global memory: 100X access time

Register Spilling: register allocation exceed available register. Allocation moves to global memory (overhead).

Memory Coalescing: Threads in a warp access contiguous memory; Use vectorized load float4/float8.

Prefetch: Load data for next computation before current computation; Load takes place in parallel.

Bank conflict: Shared memory is divided into banks. If multiple threads access the same bank, it causes serialization. Use padding/interleave memory access.

Asynchronous copy and prefetch: Use async_work_group_copy to move data from global to shared memory without stalling execution

Use warp intrinsics (shuffle_xor, reduce_over_group) to reduce global memory dependence.

Problem 1: REDUCTION: Sum/Min/Max optimization on GPU

Problem: Given N elements, find the sum or minimum or maximum of all elements.

On a serialized optimal algorithm, time complexity will be O(N). By default, each thread can load one element and at each step, each thread can sum 2 elements and number of active threads will reduce by 1.

As there is 1 operation per thread, the operation is **memory bound**.

Core idea with example:

If N=16, start with 8 threads and stride=8 and reduce number of threads and strides by 2 at each step till one element remains.

Note: the processing done of each thread.

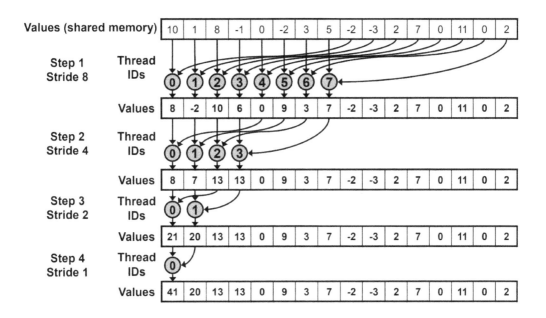

Highly optimized GPU reduction approach:

- 2D Input of size NxN
- Block size is B. Then, number of grids/tiles = N^2/B
- Create array of size B in shared memory (to store result from B threads).
- Each thread will load and reduce multiple elements by incrementing strides (1,2,4,8,...) to increase **arithmetic intensity per thread**.
- For each thread with local thread id **tid**:
  - [**reduction while loading data into shared memory**]
  - Global id **gid** = Block id * **2B** + **tid**
  - Load 2 elements with index **gid** and **gid+B**
  - Store the sum in shared memory in index **tid**
  - Continue previous 2 steps of loading and sum by incrementing gid by **grid_size** (= 2B * grid_id) till end of N^2 is reached.
- Synchronize threads to ensure shared memory is prepared. [**overhead but first reduction took place**]
- Number of active threads reduce as iterations take place.
- Start reducing with stride = **B/2 till 32** (reducing by factor of 2 at each step).
  - Strided index + reverse loop is used.
  - Add value at index **tid+stride** to current sum.

- o **Reverse loop reduces bank conflict** (accessing memory in same bank/close to each other)
  - o **Synchronize** after every iteration.
- If block size B = 512 (fixed for a GPU), **unroll above loop when stride <= B**.
  - o So, if B>512 and tid<256, sum elements at index tid and tid+256 and then, synchronize.
  - o If B>256 and tid<128, sum elements at index tid and tid+128 and synchronize.
  - o Continue till stride 64.
- **For stride <= 32**:
  - o 32 is wrap size so threads are in wrap and **No synchronization is needed as wrap works in lockstep**
  - o If **tid < 32 (wrap size)**, unroll loop and compute sum of elements at index tid, tid+1, tid+2, tid+4, tid+8, …, tid+32 (strides 1 to 32).
- Thread with tid 0 will write the final result in an array in global memory with index block_id.
- The array in global memory can be reduced further in **GPU as a separate kernel** or if it is same enough, it can run on **CPU**.

Parallel reduction complexity

- N elements.
- **O(logN)** reduction steps.
- Each step S does **O(N/2^S)**. Amount of work reduces each step.
- With P parallel cores, time complexity = O(N/P + logN)
  - o In a thread block N=P so O(logN).

Problem 2: SCAN: Prefix Sum optimization on GPU

Prefix sum is defined as element at index "I" should be the sum of all elements in input array before it (that is index 0 to I). If I is included, it is known as "**inclusive scan**" or else "**exclusive scan**".

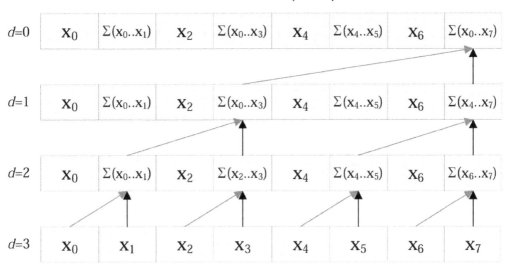

Phase 1: UP SWEEP (REDUCE)

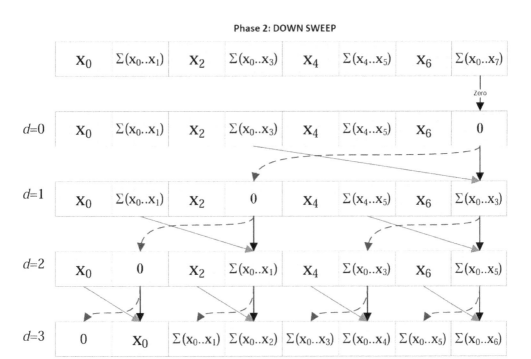

Phase 2: DOWN SWEEP

Basic idea: Every number is a sum of power of 2s.

Highly optimized GPU scan approach:

- 1D input of size B.
- Create a temporary array in shared memory.
- Current thread id = **tid**. Each thread will **create 2 outputs** at index **2*tid** and **2*tid+1** (in case of exclusive scan).
- Load 2 input elements at index **2*tid** and **2*tid+1**
- **Phase 1** (logN steps; in step I, 2^I threads are used):
  - Synchronize so all elements are loaded/updated.
  - Current elements A (index **offset*(2*tid+1)-1**) and B (index **offset*(2*tid+2)-1**). Gap is 1 (=2^0) initially so A_{index} = 2*tid and B_{index} = 2*tid+1.
  - **Add A to B and update B** in shared memory.
  - **Increase gap by factor of 2**. A (index offset*(2*tid+1)-1) and B (at index: offset*(2*tid+2)-1). Gap is offset. Offset *= 2.
- Set last element to 0 (exclusive scan).
- **Phase 2**: (Separate kernel launch: Reverse of Phase 1)
  - Synchronize.
  - Reduce offset by a factor of 2 (use offset of phase 1).
  - Current elements A (index **offset*(2*tid+1)-1**) and B (index **offset*(2*tid+2)-1**).
  - Set B = A + B
  - Set A = original value of B.
- Synchronize.
- Final output at index **2*tid** and **2*tid+1** is moved to global memory.

Note: In phase 2, each element is loaded by 2 threads in each iteration -> **2-way bank conflict** -> 2 serialized memory access [**performance overhead**].

The offsets can be adjusted to avoid bank conflict.

Problem 3: Sliding Window Optimization on GPU

Sliding window:

- Input of size NxN
- Window of size KxK

- For every sub-matrix in input of the size of window, compute max or average.
- Place the output at the same index as the index of the top left corner of the current window.
- Brute force approach: $O(N^2K^2)$ time. Each output invokes $O(K^2)$ memory transfer to shared memory.

Core concepts in implementing sliding window efficiently in GPU:

- Work Distribution & Execution Model
    - Work-item: **Each thread computes one output value** corresponding to a window position.
    - Workgroup (Block): Entire output is split into smaller contiguous components of size **TILE_H × TILE_W** and each tile is assigned to a block.
    - Tile size depends on register pressure, block size, shared memory size.
    - ND-Range: **SHIFT_H × SHIFT_W** stride values are considered.
- Memory Access Optimization
    - For a block, the required input of size **(TILE_H + WINDOW_H - 1) × (TILE_W + WINDOW_W - 1)** is loaded into **shared memory**.
    - **Each thread loads a separate part of the region (not the entire window)**. There is no redundant global memory access.
    - **Vectorized loads** (float4) are used to reduce memory bandwidth by a factor of 4.
    - Memory is **prefetched** into shared memory while sum is computed.
- Computation Optimization
    - Uses **SIMD (vec<float,4>)** for summation.
- Memory Write Optimization
    - Each thread needs to write its output to global memory.
    - **Global Memory writes are coalesced** results in one write per block.

C++ code snippet using SYCL:

```
constexpr int WINDOW_H = 6;
constexpr int WINDOW_W = 6;
constexpr int TILE_H = 8;
constexpr int TILE_W = 8;
constexpr int SHIFT_H = 4;
```

```
constexpr int SHIFT_W = 4;

void sliding_window_2D(queue &q, buffer<float, 2> &input, buffer<float, 2>
&output, int H, int W) {
    q.submit([&](handler &h) {
        accessor in(input, h, read_only);
        accessor out(output, h, write_only, no_init);

        h.parallel_for(nd_range<2>({(H - WINDOW_H) / SHIFT_H, (W - WINDOW_W) /
SHIFT_W}, {TILE_H, TILE_W}),
            [=](nd_item<2> item) {
                int gid_x = item.get_group(1) * SHIFT_W;
                int gid_y = item.get_group(0) * SHIFT_H;
                int lid_x = item.get_local_id(1);
                int lid_y = item.get_local_id(0);

                // Shared memory for a tile + window overlap
                local_accessor<float, 2> smem(range<2>(TILE_H + WINDOW_H - 1,
TILE_W + WINDOW_W - 1), item.get_group());

                // Load input into shared memory (avoiding redundant loads)
                for (int i = lid_y; i < TILE_H + WINDOW_H - 1; i += TILE_H) {
                    for (int j = lid_x; j < TILE_W + WINDOW_W - 1; j += TILE_W)
{
                        int y = gid_y + i;
                        int x = gid_x + j;
                        smem[i][j] = (y < H && x < W) ? in[y][x] : 0;
                    }
                }
                item.barrier(access::fence_space::local_space);

                // Compute sum for each sliding window using vectorized loads
with remainder handling
                float sum = 0.0f;
                int remainder = WINDOW_W % 4;
                for (int i = 0; i < WINDOW_H; i++) {
                    int j;
                    for (j = 0; j <= WINDOW_W - 4; j += 4) {
                        sycl::vec<float, 4> vec = *reinterpret_cast<const
sycl::vec<float, 4>*>(&smem[lid_y + i][lid_x + j]);
                        sum += vec[0] + vec[1] + vec[2] + vec[3];
                    }
                    // Handle remainder elements if WINDOW_W is not a multiple
of 4
                    for (; j < WINDOW_W; j++) {
                        sum += smem[lid_y + i][lid_x + j];
                    }
                }

                // Store the output using coalesced writes
                if (gid_y + lid_y < H - WINDOW_H && gid_x + lid_x < W -
WINDOW_W) {
```

```
                    out[gid_y + lid_y][gid_x + lid_x] = sum / (WINDOW_H *
WINDOW_W);
            }
        });
    });
}
```

Problem 4: MatMul implementation on GPU

Concepts/Optimizations used:

- **Each thread calculates one output element.** So, for NxN output, there are NxN threads.
- **Tiling with Shared Memory**: Reduces global memory accesses by loading matrix blocks into shared memory.
- **Vectorized Memory Loads (float4=vector width of 128 bits so can store 4 FP32 at once)**: Improves memory bandwidth efficiency.
- **Warp-Level Reduction**: Uses intra-warp summation for faster accumulation.
- **Prefetching Tiles**: Loads the next tile while computing the current tile.
- **Memory Coalescing**: Ensures efficient global memory access patterns.
- **Loop Unrolling**: Reduces instruction overhead for better performance.

C++ code snippet using SYCL:

```
constexpr int TILE_SIZE = 16;
constexpr int VECTOR_WIDTH = 4;   // Vectorized loads (float4)

void matmul_optimized(queue &q, float *A, float *B, float *C, int N) {
    buffer<float, 2> bufA(A, range<2>(N, N));
    buffer<float, 2> bufB(B, range<2>(N, N));
    buffer<float, 2> bufC(C, range<2>(N, N));

    q.submit([&](handler &h) {
        accessor<float, 2, access::mode::read> accA(bufA, h);
        accessor<float, 2, access::mode::read> accB(bufB, h);
        accessor<float, 2, access::mode::write> accC(bufC, h);

        // Shared memory for tiling
        local_accessor<float, 2> tileA(range<2>(TILE_SIZE, TILE_SIZE),
h);
        local_accessor<float, 2> tileB(range<2>(TILE_SIZE, TILE_SIZE),
h);
```

59

```
        h.parallel_for(nd_range<2>({N, N}, {TILE_SIZE, TILE_SIZE})),
[=](nd_item<2> item) {
            int row = item.get_global_id(0);
            int col = item.get_global_id(1);
            int localRow = item.get_local_id(0);
            int localCol = item.get_local_id(1);
            int groupRow = item.get_group(0);
            int groupCol = item.get_group(1);

            float sum = 0.0f;
            float nextTileA[TILE_SIZE], nextTileB[TILE_SIZE];

            // Prefetch first tile
            for (int j = 0; j < TILE_SIZE; j += VECTOR_WIDTH) {
                auto vecA = *(sycl::vec<float, VECTOR_WIDTH>
*)(&accA[row][j]);
                auto vecB = *(sycl::vec<float, VECTOR_WIDTH>
*)(&accB[j][col]);
                for (int k = 0; k < VECTOR_WIDTH; ++k) {
                    nextTileA[j + k] = vecA[k];
                    nextTileB[j + k] = vecB[k];
                }
            }

            // Loop over tiles
            for (int t = 0; t < N / TILE_SIZE; ++t) {
                // Swap buffers
                float prevTileA[TILE_SIZE], prevTileB[TILE_SIZE];
                for (int j = 0; j < TILE_SIZE; ++j) {
                    prevTileA[j] = nextTileA[j];
                    prevTileB[j] = nextTileB[j];
                }

                // Prefetch next tile
                if (t + 1 < N / TILE_SIZE) {
                    for (int j = 0; j < TILE_SIZE; j += VECTOR_WIDTH) {
                        auto vecA = *(sycl::vec<float, VECTOR_WIDTH>
*)(&accA[row][(t + 1) * TILE_SIZE + j]);
                        auto vecB = *(sycl::vec<float, VECTOR_WIDTH>
*)(&accB[(t + 1) * TILE_SIZE + j][col]);
                        for (int k = 0; k < VECTOR_WIDTH; ++k) {
                            nextTileA[j + k] = vecA[k];
                            nextTileB[j + k] = vecB[k];
                        }
                    }
                }
```

```cpp
                // Load into shared memory
                tileA[localRow][localCol] = prevTileA[localCol];
                tileB[localRow][localCol] = prevTileB[localRow];

                item.barrier(access::fence_space::local_space);

                // Compute partial sum
                #pragma unroll
                for (int k = 0; k < TILE_SIZE; ++k) {
                    sum += tileA[localRow][k] * tileB[k][localCol];
                }

                item.barrier(access::fence_space::local_space);
            }

            // Warp reduction (assumes TILE_SIZE <= 32)
            for (int offset = TILE_SIZE / 2; offset > 0; offset /= 2) {
                sum += item.sub_group_broadcast(sum, offset);
            }

            // Store result
            if (localRow == 0) {
                accC[row][col] = sum;
            }
        });
    }).wait();
}
```

CPU architecture (for parallel workload)

Modern CPU follow a NUMA (Non-uniform memory access) architecture:

This is a **CCD (Core Chiplet Die)**:

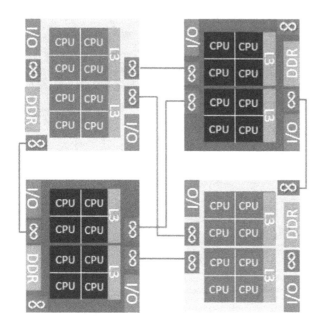

CCD has 4 **CCX (Core CompleX)**:

A CPU will have 2 to 4 CCD (so total number of cores will be 64 to 128).

For optimizing a workload on CPU:

- Number of cores in CPU (64 to **128**) is significantly less than GPU (~**2048**).
- Use **pthread_setaffinity_np**() to bind threads to specific cores.
- Partition and allocate memory near threads in same NUMA node or adjacent NUMA node (not diagonal one) using **mbind**.
- Pin threads to NUMA nodes for better cache locality.
- Minimize inter-NUMA communication.

- Use NUMA-aware locks or lock-free structures to avoid contention.
- Optimize work distribution based on NUMA topology.
- Analyze performance using **numactl** (NUMA topology), **numastat** (monitor memory access), **hwloc-ls** (core affinity and cache hierarchy), **VTune** (NUMA memory access pattern).

Workload runs on CPU instead of GPU when:

- Size of the workload is small or it cannot be broken down into a large number of independent threads (< 1024).
- GPU processes the large workload and creates a smaller intermediate data which is most efficient to execute on CPU.

Single thread performance on CPU is significantly better than GPU.

This gives rise of **heterogeneous computing** where parts of the workload runs on different available processors (like GPU, CPU, TPU and more).

DL Software Stack

Understanding how to use DL practically gives an unfair advantage.

On **CPU** (for DL inference):

- Choose a DL framework: **TensorFlow** or **PyTorch**
- Choose a CPU server: Intel **Xeon 6** CPU or AMD Ryzen8 CPU
- Build software stack with an efficient compiler: **ICC** (for Intel CPU), **AOCC** (for AMD CPU). Ensure all ISA is enabled (like **AVX512 VNNI**).
- Choose OS: **Ubuntu, SElinux**
- CPU Inference Library: Enable **OneDNN** (for Intel CPU) and **ZenDNN** (for AMD CPU). These provide optimized kernel implementations (link with framework).
- For efficient algebraic routines, use **EIGEN** or **AMD-BLIS** or **MKL**.
- Enable **Intel Optimized OpenMP** or **Intel TBB** (for parallel workloads).
- Enable **TCMalloc** (for efficient memory allocation) and **FBGEMM** (for efficient low precision GEMMs).
- For profiling, **Tracing** tools (**Tensorboard** by TF to check op level timings), (for capturing ISA), **AMD uProf**, **gprof** (for AMD CPU), **VTune** (for Intel CPU), native tools like **htop**.

For training, we do not recommend CPU though it is theoretically possible but infeasible for most modern DL workloads.

On **GPU** (for training and inference):

- Choose a DL framework: **TensorFlow** or **PyTorch**
- Choose a GPU: **NVIDIA A100/H100** with NVLink/PCIe (for training or inference); For inference, consider specialized AI accelerators like **Intel Gaudi**.
- Choose OS: **Ubuntu**
- Use accelerator libraries for efficient kernels: **cuDNN**, **TensorRT**
- For efficient algebraic routines, use **cuBLAS**, **cuSPARSE**, Thrust, cuFFT.

- Use **NCCL** (NVIDIA Collective Communications Library) for **optimized GPU routines** like reduction, scan.
- Use **SYCL** or **CUDA** (Compute Unified Device Architecture) for **writing custom efficient kernels** on GPU.
- For processing and loading data, use library **DALI** (NVIDIA Data Loading Library)
- For deployment, use **NVIDIA Triton** to optimize DL model serving for maximum GPU utilization.
- For performance analysis, use **nvProf**, **NVIDIA Nsight**, CUDA-GDB, CUDA-MEMCHECK. Use **DLProf** to check GPU utilization.

DL breakthroughs Timeline

Short timeline of breakthroughs in DL:

- 1943: Perceptron
- 1958: MLP
- 1975: Backpropagation
- 1982: RNN
- 1995: CNN
- 1997: LSTM
- 2005: GPU
- 2012: AlexNet
- 2015: ResNet50
- 2017: Transformer, BERT, LLM
- 2018: GPT-1
- 2021: DALL-E, Stable Diffusion

Deep Learning model list [Applications]

These are the major category of Deep Learning models that are used in practice. Each category has multiple variants and can be applied on multiple domains.

Model Category	Strengths / Problems It Can Solve	Weaknesses
Multi-Layer Perceptron (MLP)	For fixed-length, structured input data. Good baseline for many classification/regression tasks.	Cannot capture spatial or sequential patterns without engineered features. Limited capacity for handling complex data like images or audio.
Convolutional Neural Network (CNN)	Excellent at capturing local patterns (like edges in images, local correlations in audio/text). Highly efficient for spatial data tasks. Translation (rotation) invariant due to weight sharing.	Not designed to capture long-range or sequential dependencies.
Recurrent Neural Network (RNN)	Designed to process sequential data (language, time series). For tasks where order matters. Handles variable-length sequences.	Prone to vanishing/exploding gradient problems. Struggles with long-term dependencies. Slow due to sequential processing.
Long Short-Term Memory Network (LSTM)	Solved gradient problems of RNN. Effective for capturing long-term dependencies in sequences.	Computationally more expensive than RNN. Still processes data sequentially, leading to slower training/inference on long sequences.
Transformers	Highly parallelizable. Captures long-range dependencies via self-attention.	Requires large amounts of data and compute resources. Quadratic complexity with respect to sequence length

		can be limiting. Less interpretable.
Encoder-only Transformer (BERT)	Excellent for understanding context in input text (classification, extraction tasks). Provides rich contextual embeddings.	Not designed for text generation since they lack a decoding mechanism. Primarily suited for understanding rather than generating language.
Decoder-only Transformer (LLM) (GPT-3/4, LLaMA)	Very effective for text generation, conversation, and zero/few-shot tasks. Can generate coherent, context-aware responses.	Computationally expensive, especially at large scales. Without an encoder, may struggle with certain understanding tasks without proper prompting.
Encoder-Decoder Transformers (LLMs) (T5, BART)	Ideal for sequence-to-sequence tasks like translation, summarization, paraphrasing. Combines understanding and generation in one architecture.	Training and inference are more resource-intensive.
Small Language Model (SLM) (distilled versions of Transformers like DistilBERT/TinyBERT)	Offer a good balance between performance and efficiency. Suitable for resource-constrained environments (mobile).	May exhibit lower accuracy compared to LLM. Require careful distillation to preserve performance.
Two-Tower / Siamese Networks	Efficient for matching and retrieval tasks (like recommendation, similarity search). Separately encodes two different input types (like users and songs).	Requires careful design of similarity measures and fusion strategies. May miss complex interactions between the two towers unless further processing is applied.

	Trained 2 different models (CNN, BERT) together so image and text embedding are in same representation. Output of different models can be comparable.	Complex training process using CLIP.
Multi-modal model		
Multi-task model	Can solve multiple problems using a single model. Leverages knowledge in solving one problem to solve another problem.	More training time as multiple output is involved.
Graph Neural Networks (GNN)	Model relationships and interactions in graph-structured data (social networks, molecular structures, recommendation systems). Captures both local and global structure.	Can be computationally intensive on very large graphs. Often requires domain-specific tuning and careful design of the graph structure.

There are other variants as CNN based encoder and decoder for tasks like super image resolution.

Following is the list of popular Deep Learning models that are tailored for specific applications. These are extensively used in preparing Deep Learning System Design:

Model	Task	Input / Output Data	Example Use Case
MLP (Multi-Layer Perceptron)	Basic Classification / Regression	**Input:** Fixed-length feature vectors (can be concatenated embeddings from various sources).	Combining user and song embeddings to predict the likelihood of a click or like.

		Output: Scalar predictions or class probabilities via FC layers.	
Fusion Layer	Combining Multi-Modal/Source Embeddings	**Input:** Two or more embedding vectors (e.g., user tower + song tower).	Merging user preferences with song features in a two-tower recommendation model.
		Output: A fused embedding (via concatenation, weighted sum, or attention) used for final scoring.	
FC + Softmax / Sigmoid	Classification Head	**Input:** Fused embedding or feature vector.	Final decision layer to classify a tweet as toxic/non-toxic or rank recommended songs.
		Output: Class probabilities (Softmax for multi-class; Sigmoid for binary decisions).	
Two-Tower / Dual-Encoder Model	Matching & Ranking	**Input:** Two sets of embeddings (e.g., user embedding from one tower and song embedding from the other).	Matching a user's taste to candidate songs in a recommendation system.
		Output: Similarity score (typically using cosine similarity or dot product).	
CNN for Image (ResNet50, YOLO for object detection)	Image Feature Extraction	**Input:** Raw image of fixed size.	Extract features from an image for image recognition.
		Output: Embedding vector (e.g., 256D) of features.	

CNN for Audio Features (WaveNet, MelGAN)	Audio Feature Extraction	**Input:** Raw audio signals or spectrograms (sequential data capturing time-frequency patterns).	Converting a song's mel spectrogram into an embedding to capture rhythm and melody.
		Output: Fixed-length song embedding vector (e.g., 256D) capturing musical characteristics.	
BERT-NER (SpaCy, Flair)	Named Entity Recognition (NER)	**Input:** Unstructured text (like tweets, reviews)	Extracting entities like artist names or event locations from text.
		Output: List of detected entities with labels (like "Eminem" as ARTIST, "Coachella" as EVENT)	
BERTopic (LDA, NMF, Top2Vec)	Topic Modeling	**Input:** A corpus of documents (song lyrics, reviews)	Grouping songs by abstract themes like "chill vibes".
		Output: Topic clusters with representative keywords (like a cluster labeled "metal rap")	
RoBERTa / DistilBERT (ALBERT, ELECTRA)	Text Classification	**Input:** Short-to-moderate text (tweets, reviews).	Classifying tweets as toxic or non-toxic in a moderation system.
		Output: Class probabilities or contextual embeddings (e.g., toxic vs. non-toxic scores).	

T5 / Pegasus (BART, mT5)	Text Summarization / Paraphrasing	**Input:** Long-form text (album reviews, long comments)	Summarizing detailed user reviews into a brief digest. Balancing text dataset.
		Output: A concise summary or a paraphrased version of the input text.	
SimCSE / Sentence-BERT (Universal Sentence Encoder, LaBSE)	Sentence Embeddings for Similarity Search	**Input:** Short text snippets (song descriptions, queries).	Matching a user query to similar song descriptions or finding similar lyrical themes.
		Output: Dense fixed-length vectors (like 768D embeddings)	
DeepFM / Wide & Deep (xDeepFM, DCN)	CTR Prediction / Ranking	**Input:** Structured/tabular data (user demographics, historical clicks, categorical features).	Predicting the likelihood that a user will click on a recommended song.
		Output: Scalar scores (predicted click-through rates or ranking scores).	
BiLSTM / Transformer XL (TimeSformer, Hawkes Processes)	Temporal Sequence Modeling	**Input:** Sequential data (time-ordered list of songs in a user's listening history).	Modeling a user's shifting taste over time or throughout the day.
		Output: Contextualized sequence embedding reflecting evolving user preferences.	

Graph Neural Networks (GCN, GAT, PinSAGE) (GraphSAGE, RGAT)	Graph-Based Relationship Learning	**Input:** Graph-structured data (nodes: songs/artists; edges: collaborations or similarity).	Recommending new songs based on artist collaborations or similar genres.
		Output: Node embeddings that capture relationship strengths.	
DistilBERT / TinyBERT (MobileBERT, ALBERT)	Efficient Transformer Inference	**Input:** Text data (similar to BERT but optimized for low compute).	Running text classification (e.g., toxic tweet detection) on edge devices.
		Output: Compact contextual embeddings or classification scores.	
Generative Models (GPT-4, LLaMA, DeepSeek)	Text Generation / Zero/Few-Shot Tasks	**Input:** Text prompt.	Generating natural language explanations for recommendations or summarizing user histories.
		Output: Generated text or explanations; may also provide embeddings for retrieval tasks.	

Training & Inference time of DL models

Following table summarizes the training time, fine-tuning time for a pre-trained model and inference time for a select popular DL models to give you a rough estimate to discuss on training/inference time:

Model	Training Time (Dataset & GPUs)	Inference Time (Input Size & Hardware)
ResNet50	**From Scratch:** ~1–2 days on 4 GPUs (ImageNet, ~14M images **Fine-tuning:** ~30 minutes on 4 GPUs (100K images)	**CPU:** ~1–20 ms per image (~50–100 images/s) **GPU:** ~0.1–0.2 ms per image (1,000+ images/s)
BERT	**From Scratch:** ~4–5 days on 16 GPUs (≈3.3B tokens) **Fine-tuning:** ~30–60 minutes on 1 GPU (100K text examples)	**CPU:** ~20–30 ms per sentence **GPU:** ~5–10 ms per sentence (200+ sentences/s)
DistilBERT (Lightweight transformer)	**From Scratch:** ~2–3 days on 8 GPUs (if training a distilled model from scratch) **Fine-tuning:** ~20–30 minutes on 1 GPU (100K text examples)	**CPU:** ~10–15 ms per sentence **GPU:** ~3–5 ms per sentence (2–3× faster than full BERT)
LSTM	**From Scratch:** ~1–2 hours on 1 GPU (100K sequences) **Fine-tuning:** ~45–60 minutes on 1 GPU (100K sequences)	**CPU:** ~30–40 ms per sequence **GPU:** ~10–15 ms per sequence
RNN (vanilla)	**From Scratch:** ~1–2 hours on 1 GPU (100K sequences) **Fine-tuning:** ~40–50 minutes on 1 GPU (100K sequences)	**CPU:** ~30 ms per sequence **GPU:** ~10 ms per sequence

T5 (base)	**From Scratch:** ~2–3 weeks on 8 GPUs (trained on massive corpora, e.g., >100M examples **Fine-tuning:** ~2–3 hours on 4 GPUs (100K examples)	**CPU:** ~300–500 ms per sequence **GPU:** ~50–100 ms per sequence (due to decoding/generation overhead)
GPT-4 (Decoder-only LLM)	**From Scratch:** Several weeks on thousands of GPUs (massive scale, not feasible in most settings) **Fine-tuning:** ~12–24 hours on 8 GPUs (for a smaller variant, 100K examples)	**GPU:** ~500 ms to 1 s per prompt Throughput: a few queries per second (high compute required)
LLaMA (7B)	**From Scratch:** ~3–4 days on 8 GPUs (approximate for a mid-sized model) **Fine-tuning:** ~3–4 hours on 4–8 GPUs (100K examples)	**GPU:** ~50–100 ms per prompt Throughput: ~20–30 queries per second on high-end GPUs

Perceptron [1943]

Perceptron is the basic building block of Deep Learning. It tries to learn a **linear function** that is the equation **X = YB+C** (where B, C are constants).

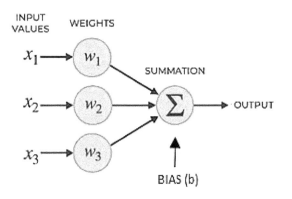

This is the formula:

$$y = \sum_{i=1}^{N} x_i * w_i + B$$

Note This is the equation of a **straight line in N dimensional space**.

The concept was formed by Warren McCulloch and Walter Pitts in **1943**. It was implemented in a hardware in January **1957** by Frank Rosenblatt.

This is a vector multiplication mathematically:

Y = B + X^T W

- Y is output
- X^T is transpose of matrix X (inputs).
- W is weights.
- B is bias

Perceptron can solve all linear problems that follow a linear relationship between input and output. Perceptron can:

- Learn **AND** and **OR** gates
- Real life problems like:
    - Predicting pass / fail grades
    - Loan approval (if income > threshold)

76

- o Spam email (if specific words like "free" occur beyond a threshold)
- Problems it cannot solve:
  - o Cannot learn **XOR** gate
  - o Predicting more than 2 grades (A, B, C, D, …)
  - o Image recognition (non-linear patterns)

Linear layer (nn.linear)

In Deep Learning models, perceptron is referred to as Linear layer.

Feature	Linear Layer (nn.Linear)
Operation	Performs $Y = XW^T + b$ (Matrix Multiplication + Bias Addition)
Bias Term	Bias b is trainable/learnable parameter.
Used In	Neural Networks (MLP, CNN, RNN, etc.)
Autograd Support	Yes, optimized for backpropagation

During training, W and b is learnt.

X is the input and Y is the output during inference.

Perceptron with step function

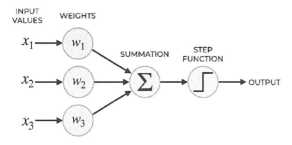

$$y = step\left(\sum_{i=1}^{N} x_i * w_i + B \right)$$

$$step(x) = \begin{cases} 1 & \text{if } x \geq 0 \\ 0 & \text{if } x < 0 \end{cases}$$

step() is the step function.

Step function helps the perceptron find more complex equations. The idea is if we add linear lines, we get a resultant linear line. The equation stays same.

Line$_1$ + Line$_2$ + ... + Line$_N$ = Line$_M$

With the step function, perceptron is able to learn most complex polynomial equations beyond a straight line.

Observe this:

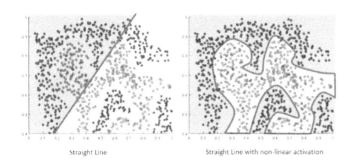

Straight Line   Straight Line with non-linear activation

This can solve basic tasks like **Predicting score of a student using past scores**.

In such networks:

- X is the input data.
- W is the weight which determines if the neural network works correctly. This is calculated while training the model.

Additional problems that can be solved:

- XOR gate
- Can handle more complex patterns than just one perceptron for problems like weather prediction, loan approval (non-linear risk assessment)

Single Layer Neural Network

A perceptron had one output but it can be modified to produce 2 outputs.

This can be seen as 2 labels and the output will be probability a particular label is the answer.

This makes Perceptron solve basic classification tasks like **predicting if a stock will rise or fall** based on some input parameters.

Perceptron with 2 inputs:

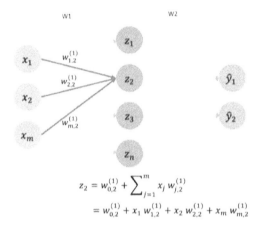

$$z_2 = w_{0,2}^{(1)} + \sum_{j=1}^{m} x_j \, w_{j,2}^{(1)}$$
$$= w_{0,2}^{(1)} + x_1 \, w_{1,2}^{(1)} + x_2 \, w_{2,2}^{(1)} + x_m \, w_{m,2}^{(1)}$$

Simplified as:

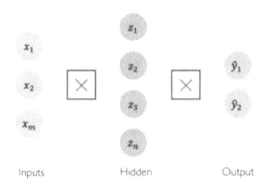

Inputs   Hidden   Output

This is a **single layer Neural Network**.

Multi-Layer Perception (MLP) / Neural Network [1958]

In MLP, there are multiple perceptrons stacked together in different layers.

These are more powerful and can solve tasks like **Digit Recognition from an image**.

Each hidden layer has its own set of weights and takes input as the output of the previous layer.

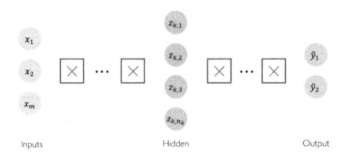

Problems that **MLP can solve**:

Problem Type	Why MLP Works?
XOR Function	Can model non-linear relationships.
Digit Recognition (MNIST)	Learns patterns in pixel intensities.
Speech Emotion Classification	Learns patterns in frequency features of speech.
Handwritten Character Recognition	Works well with features like pixel intensities or edge detection.
Sentiment Analysis on Short Text	Works if input is converted into meaningful numerical vectors.
Medical Diagnosis (Predicting Disease from Symptoms)	Can learn complex relationships in patient data.
Fraud Detection (Credit Card Fraud)	Can identify complex fraudulent patterns in transactions.

Predicting House Prices	Learns non-linear dependencies between features like location, size, and amenities.
Stock Market Movement Prediction	Can capture short-term non-linear relationships, but performance is limited.
Image Classification (Simple Datasets like CIFAR-10)	Works for simple classification but struggles with complex images without convolutional layers.

Problems where **MLP will struggle to solve**:

Problem Type	Why MLP Fails?	Alternative Approach
Sequence Prediction (e.g., Next Word Prediction, Machine Translation)	Cannot handle sequential dependencies.	**RNNs, LSTMs, Transformers**
Long-Distance Dependencies (Understanding Context in Long Sentences)	Struggles to retain information over long input sequences.	**Transformers (BERT, GPT)**
Time-Series Forecasting (Stock Prices, Weather, Sales)	MLP treats inputs independently, ignoring temporal patterns.	**LSTMs, Transformers**
Object Detection in Images	Does not learn spatial hierarchies.	**CNNs (YOLO, Faster R-CNN)**
Image Segmentation (Identifying Objects in an Image)	Lacks spatial feature extraction.	**U-Net, CNNs**
Graph-Based Problems (Social Networks, Molecule Prediction)	Cannot process relational data.	**Graph Neural Networks (GNNs)**

Reinforcement Learning Tasks (Self-Driving Cars)	Cannot model sequential decision-making.	Deep Q-Learning, Policy Gradient Methods
Recommender Systems	Fails when most inputs are missing or categorical.	Matrix Factorization, Transformers
High-Resolution Image Generation	Struggles with realistic feature generation.	GANs, Diffusion Models

This is an example **Python code using PyTorch** DL framework for creating a **simple MLP (2 linear layers)** along with training and inference phases:

```python
import torch
import torch.nn as nn
import torch.optim as optim

# Define a simple MLP
class MLP(nn.Module):
    def __init__(self):
        super().__init__()
        self.fc = nn.Sequential(
            nn.Linear(2, 4), nn.ReLU(),
            nn.Linear(4, 1), nn.Sigmoid()
        )

    def forward(self, x):
        return self.fc(x)

# Create model, loss, and optimizer
model = MLP()
criterion = nn.BCELoss()   # Binary Cross-Entropy Loss
optimizer = optim.SGD(model.parameters(), lr=0.1)

# Dummy training data (XOR problem)
X = torch.tensor([[0,0], [0,1], [1,0], [1,1]],
dtype=torch.float32)
```

84

```
Y = torch.tensor([[0], [1], [1], [0]], dtype=torch.float32)

# Train the model
for _ in range(1000):
    optimizer.zero_grad()
    loss = criterion(model(X), Y)
    loss.backward()
    optimizer.step()

# Inference
with torch.no_grad():
    print(model(X).round())  # Expected output: [[0], [1],
[1], [0]]
```

Sigmoid is an activation function used for binary classification problem (0 or 1).

RNN & LSTM [1982, 1997]

MLP and **CNN** can remember previous inputs (not fit for sequential tasks). This is solved by **RNN**.

RNN = Recurrent Neural Network

Tasks which RNNs can solve:

- Sequence to sequence (price forecasting)
- Sequence to vector (detecting positive or negative sentiment)
- Vector to sequence (image captioning)
- Encoder Decoder (text translation)

Basic formula of RNN:

$$h_t = \tanh(W_h h_{t-1} + W_x x_t + b)$$

- x_t = input at time t (dimension D)
- h_{t-1} and h_t = hidden state at time t-1 and t respectively (dimension H)
- W_h and W_x = weight matrix of size (H, H) and (H, D) respectively
- b = bias of size H
- y_t = output of size O

This is the RNN architecture:

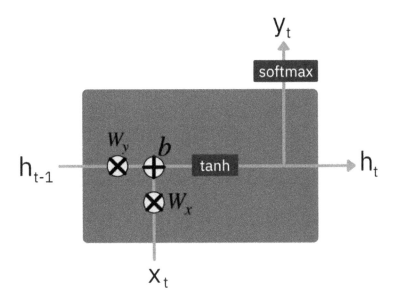

It has one cell. It can be visualized in an unrolled fashion having multiple cells one after another. The SoftMax to generate the output is optional.

For **training an RNN**:

- Backpropagation through time (BPTT) is used.
- Network output is calculated in unrolled form.
- Loss and gradient are calculated.
- Weight of RNN cell is updated.

Variants of RNN:

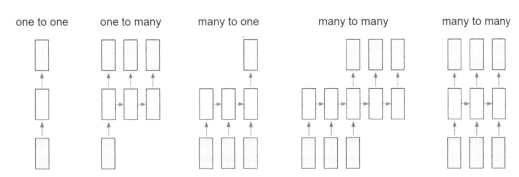

RNNs have these problems:

- **Only supports short term memory** because of vanishing gradient: while backpropagation, gradients shrink and it is impossible to learn long term dependency.
- **Exploding gradient**: Large gradient values make training unstable

Solution to short term memory: **LSTM** and **GRU**.

LSTM architecture:

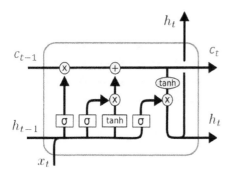

Basic formula of LSTM:

$$f_t = \sigma(W_f[h_{t-1}, x_t] + b_f)$$

$$i_t = \sigma(W_i[h_{t-1}, x_t] + b_i)$$

$$\tilde{C}_t = \tanh(W_c[h_{t-1}, x_t] + b_c)$$

$$C_t = f_t \odot C_{t-1} + i_t \odot \tilde{C}_t$$

$$o_t = \sigma(W_o[h_{t-1}, x_t] + b_o)$$

$$h_t = o_t \odot \tanh(C_t)$$

Where:

- σ = sigmoid function
- Forget Gate f_t: Determines how much past information to discard.
- Input Gate i_t: Decides how much new information to store.

88

- Cell State C_t: Stores long-term memory.
- Output Gate o_t: Controls output from memory

There are 4 weights, all of size **(H, D+H)**.

LSTM requires 4X more memory space than RNN.

Transformer Neural Network [2017]

Transformer NN addresses the problems of RNN and LSTM (slow train, difficult parallization and small context).

This is the **architecture of Transformer Neural Network**:

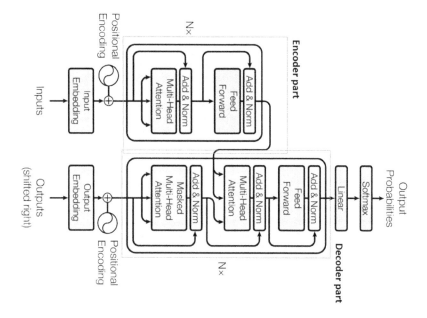

Understanding the architecture:

Consider the problem of **sequence-to-sequence task** (like English to Japanese):

Encoder part:

- Input is an English text (say batch size B =10, sentence length L = 50, Embedding size M = 512). If length of sentence < L, add **<PAD>** tokens.
- Each word is converted to a vector using pre-trained word embeddings like Word2vec (**B x L x M**).
- Positional encoding: Each word vector is added to a positional vector that captures the position of the word in the text (sin and cos-based method). (**B x L x M**)

90

- There are N attention blocks. **H heads**. Multiple heads help learn more relations.
  - Query (**Q**), Key (**K**), Value (**V**) generated using input vector. Each has size (**B x L x M/H**) using a feedforward layer.
  - Multi-head attention: It generates **H** attention vector for each word and weighted average attention vector is calculated. (final output = **B x L x M**)
  - The original word vector is added with the attention vector. This is residual link to ensure information propagates (fix vanishing gradient) and makes each word vector context aware.
- Attention output is added with original vector (residual connection). This is **normalized** for stable training. (final output = **B x L x M**)
- Above part is repeated multiple times (stacked one after another).
- Output is feed to a feedforward network followed by residual connection + normalization (final output = **B x L x M**)

Decoder part:

- Input is a start token <**START**>.
- Every word is converted to an embedding vector + position encoding is added. Size (**B x L x M**)
- **Masked-multi-head self-attention**: Only previous words are considered. Later words in sequence are masked <**MASK**>. Q, K and V vectors are generated from the input. Output size (**B x L x M**)
  - Add **look-ahead mask + padding mask** of QK to generate attention matrix of size (B x L x L). Attention matrix is multiplied by V to get final embedding of size (B x L x M).
  - Look-ahead mask to ensure it does not access possible future words (which is not yet generated).
- **Multi-head cross attention**: Uses the output vectors of previous attention (as Q) and output embedding of encoder part to generate K and V and perform attention with H heads.
  - Attention matrix is comparing words in target language to words in original sentence.

- o Only padding mask is needed as all words in original sentence is available.
  - o Output size (**B x L x M**)
- Output is passed through Layer Normalization to stabilize value and gradient.
- Above part is repeated multiple times (stacked one after another).
- Final word vectors are passed to **feedforward network, Linear and SoftMax layer**. Output for each word is a vector of size = **number of words in Japanese** (target language). Total output: (**B x L x Vocabulary Size**)
  - o The **word with highest probability** is selected as the output word. There is a separate vector for each word.
  - o Instead use a **sampling technique** to generate different output every time (like in GPT).
- Once new word is generated, all generated words are passed to the decoder part again to generate the next new word (till <**END**> token is generated).

Note: While training, the loss is not calculated for <START>, <END>, <PAD>, <MASK> tokens.

Size of input text to transformer:

- The number of words is **fixed** (512 in a standard transformer).
- It is limited due to the fixed embedding size of the positional encoding. This is needed as without positional encoding; the model has no idea of token ordering. Model is trained with this size.
- To increase this during inference, one needs to train the model from scratch again. Workaround is to clip the input or split into multiple inputs (batch).
- Smaller sentences can be used with <PAD> tokens.

Variants:

- If only encoder is used = **BERT**
- If only decoder is used = **GPT**

Attention [2017]

Attention op is the foundation of Transformer architecture. It is as important as Convolution op.

Intuition of attention as a **retrieval/search operation**:

- User has a query **Q** (say you search for a video).
- Q is matched to specific parameters (key **K**: video attributes like title, metadata) of all possible outputs.
- Best matched outputs (value **V**).

SDPA (Scaled dot product attention)

Architecture of the operation:

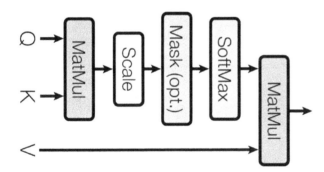

- **Size of Q**: (batch size, **N**, embedding dimension)
- **Size of K, V**: (batch size, **M**, embedding dimension); K is optional, if not provided, V is used as K.
- **Mask**: 2D tensor of size (batch size, N) (if query mask) or (batch size, M) (if value mask; do not impact output)
- N: sequence length; M: representation dimension
- **Output**: (batch size, **N**, embedding dimension) (same as input)
- Optional output: Attention matrix of size NxN.

93

- Involve 2 MatMul and 1 SoftMax.
- In modern LLM:
  - N ~ **120K**
  - E embedding dimensions = vocabulary size ~**200K**
  - M ~**100K**

BERT [2018]

BERT = **B**idirectional **E**ncoder **R**epresentations from **T**ransformers

It is a stack of encoder part of transformers.

Common tasks BERT can solve: Machine translation, Question Answering, Sentiment Analysis, Text Summarization.

To use BERT:

- Get a pre-trained BERT that understands the language.
- Fine-tune it to the specific task.

BERT BASE architecture:

- 12 "**Encoding part of a transformer**" stacked one after another.
- 1 FC + Softmax layer at the end.

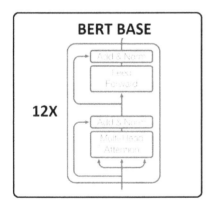

BERT Base has **110M** parameters and **BERT Large** has **340M** parameters.

Training of BERT:

- Phase 1: To make BERT understand language and context, it is trained on 2 unsupervised tasks together:
  - **Masked Language Model**: Some words are masked in input. Predict the masked words.

 DL1943 Cheatsheet: Deep Learning ©

o **Next Sentence Prediction**: Does line A follow line B?

BERT architecture as a black box with input/output:

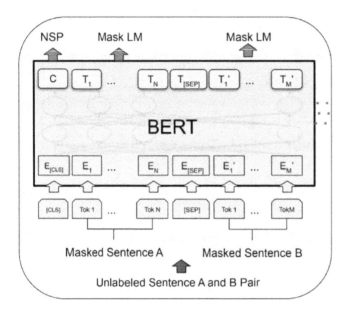

Input: 2 sentences (one of length N and other of length M).

For each sentence, few words are masked [MASK] and all words are passed as tokens. [CLS] is the starting token.

Outputs:

- First output: [C]: 0 or 1 denoting is sentence B follows sentence A conceptually.
- N tokens for sentence 1: N word vectors
- [SEP]: Separator token
- M tokens for sentence 2: M word vectors
- Note: All word vectors have the same size. Embedding at this point can be fused with other models like in 2 Tower model to perform more tasks.
- In standard BERT:
  - Each word vector is passed to a **FC + Softmax** to generate **30K output probability** (for all 30K words in vocabulary).

- Actual word will be **one hot encoding of size 30K**. One-hot encoding is a vector of size 30K with only 1 (all other 0) corresponding to the right word.
- Cross entropy loss is used to compare the probability vector and one-hot encoding vector (only for masked words)

Processing:

- Each token is converted to an embedding (like Tok1 -> E1). Each embedding is a concatenation of 3 embeddings:
    - **Token embedding**: Pre-trained embeddings (like **WordPiece**)
    - **Segment Embeddings**: Sentence number (for temporal ordering)
    - **Position embeddings**: Word number in the sentence (for ordering)

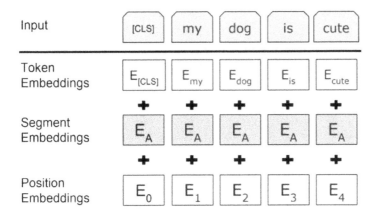

- Phase 2: Fine-tune on new task like Question Answering
    - Remove the original Fully Connected (FC) output layer
    - Add new FC layer and train it. Weights in encoders change slightly.
    - Fine-tuning is fast (~30 minutes).

Size of input in BERT = 512 token (**sequence length**) at max for standard BERT.

For input text > 512 tokens, truncate the input or split in separate 512 batch and combine results. This is due to limitations in positional encoding.

Larger variants:

- ModernBERT: **8129** sequence length

LLM [2018]

LLM architecture

- Input words -> Tokenization (N words/token when N is **sequence length**)
- **Embedding + Positional Embedding** (Each word is converted to 1D vector of size E) (size NxE).
- **Stack of decoders**
- **LayerNorm -> Linear/FC -> Softmax**
- Output probability (1D vector of probabilities of size M where M is the total number of words in the language).

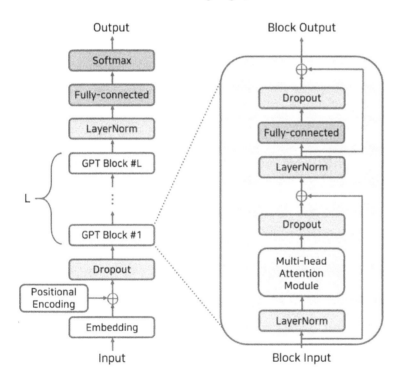

Training steps for LLM:

- Phase 1: Self-supervised learning (for language understanding): Use unannotated raw data, predict next word.
- Phase 2: Supervised learning (for instruction understanding)

99

- Phase 3: Reinforcement learning (for desired behavior)

LLM examples:

GPT-1 by OpenAI released in 2017 is the first LLM. It had 0.117B parameters.

- GPT-4/GPT-3 (by OpenAI)
- PaLM and BART (by Google)
- LLaMA (by Meta)

AlexNet [2012]

AlexNet was the first modern CNN architecture that achieved reasonable accuracy in Image Recognition task.

AlexNet architecture:

- **5 Convolution layers** (1 11x11 kernel, 3 3x3 kernel, 1 5x5 kernel)
- **3 MaxPool layers** (3 3x3 Pooling)
- **3 FC layers**
- Input is of size **3x244x244** (channels x height x width)
- Output (1D tensor of size **1000** = probability input is of class i). 1000 as ImageNet has 1000 classes.
- Number of parameters = **62.3M**
- Trained on ImageNet dataset.
- Accuracy: **Top1**: 57.1% and **Top5**: 80.2%

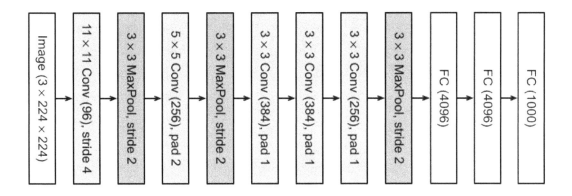

Inference:

- One forward pass (inference) of AlexNet involve **1.43 GFLOP** (floating point operations).
- Modern CPU perform at **~5.2 GFLOPs per core** (floating point operations per second).

- Modern CPU can have up to 96 cores and assuming 70% core usage, one can expect AlexNet inference to take **~4 ms** (depending on the DL software stack).
- For larger batch size like 256, core usage goes up (assume 80%). This results in **~0.8 sec**.

Training:

- Assuming the training dataset of size 50K and 20 epochs, each epoch will require 2x(50K/256) forward+backward pass. This results in **~105 minutes of training time in a single modern CPU**.

ResNet50 [2015]

Purely serial models cannot capture all features with good intensity.

Beyond AlexNet, **ResNet50** was a major breakthrough in CNN as it improved accuracy significantly by introducing the concept of residual connections.

Core improvement:

CNN are good in tracking low, mid and high-level features of images.

Stacking more Conv layers improved accuracy but it hit a limit due to vanishing gradient problem. This was resolved by ResNet by introducing residual connections. There are 2 residual connections:

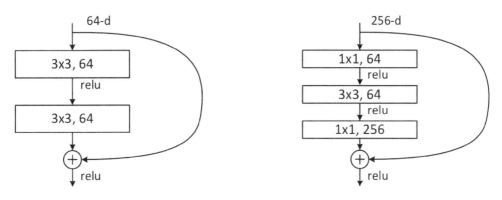

Idea: Previous output of ith op is added with the output of $(i+j)^{th}$ op. This helps the features are not lost.

ResNet50 architecture:

- **49 Convolution layers**
- 1 MaxPool
- 1 AvgPool
- 1 FC layer
- Input size: B x 3 x 244 x 244 (batch size x channel x height x width)

- Output: (1D tensor of size **1000** = probability input is of class i). 1000 as ImageNet has 1000 classes.
- Number of parameters = **23.9M**
- Trained on ImageNet dataset.
- Accuracy: **Top1**: 74.9% and **Top5**: 97%

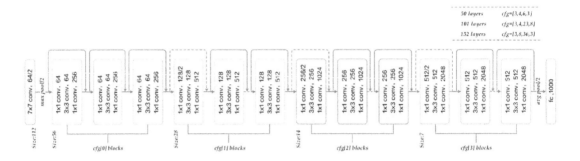

This table summarizes the different ResNet variants:

layer name	output size	18-layer	34-layer	50-layer	101-layer	152-layer
conv1	112×112	7×7, 64, stride 2				
		3×3 max pool, stride 2				
conv2_x	56×56	$\begin{bmatrix} 3\times3, 64 \\ 3\times3, 64 \end{bmatrix}\times2$	$\begin{bmatrix} 3\times3, 64 \\ 3\times3, 64 \end{bmatrix}\times3$	$\begin{bmatrix} 1\times1, 64 \\ 3\times3, 64 \\ 1\times1, 256 \end{bmatrix}\times3$	$\begin{bmatrix} 1\times1, 64 \\ 3\times3, 64 \\ 1\times1, 256 \end{bmatrix}\times3$	$\begin{bmatrix} 1\times1, 64 \\ 3\times3, 64 \\ 1\times1, 256 \end{bmatrix}\times3$
conv3_x	28×28	$\begin{bmatrix} 3\times3, 128 \\ 3\times3, 128 \end{bmatrix}\times2$	$\begin{bmatrix} 3\times3, 128 \\ 3\times3, 128 \end{bmatrix}\times4$	$\begin{bmatrix} 1\times1, 128 \\ 3\times3, 128 \\ 1\times1, 512 \end{bmatrix}\times4$	$\begin{bmatrix} 1\times1, 128 \\ 3\times3, 128 \\ 1\times1, 512 \end{bmatrix}\times4$	$\begin{bmatrix} 1\times1, 128 \\ 3\times3, 128 \\ 1\times1, 512 \end{bmatrix}\times8$
conv4_x	14×14	$\begin{bmatrix} 3\times3, 256 \\ 3\times3, 256 \end{bmatrix}\times2$	$\begin{bmatrix} 3\times3, 256 \\ 3\times3, 256 \end{bmatrix}\times6$	$\begin{bmatrix} 1\times1, 256 \\ 3\times3, 256 \\ 1\times1, 1024 \end{bmatrix}\times6$	$\begin{bmatrix} 1\times1, 256 \\ 3\times3, 256 \\ 1\times1, 1024 \end{bmatrix}\times23$	$\begin{bmatrix} 1\times1, 256 \\ 3\times3, 256 \\ 1\times1, 1024 \end{bmatrix}\times36$
conv5_x	7×7	$\begin{bmatrix} 3\times3, 512 \\ 3\times3, 512 \end{bmatrix}\times2$	$\begin{bmatrix} 3\times3, 512 \\ 3\times3, 512 \end{bmatrix}\times3$	$\begin{bmatrix} 1\times1, 512 \\ 3\times3, 512 \\ 1\times1, 2048 \end{bmatrix}\times3$	$\begin{bmatrix} 1\times1, 512 \\ 3\times3, 512 \\ 1\times1, 2048 \end{bmatrix}\times3$	$\begin{bmatrix} 1\times1, 512 \\ 3\times3, 512 \\ 1\times1, 2048 \end{bmatrix}\times3$
	1×1	average pool, 1000-d fc, softmax				
FLOPs		1.8×10^9	3.6×10^9	3.8×10^9	7.6×10^9	11.3×10^9

Each variant differs by the number of Convolution layers and the accuracy.

ResNet50 and **ResNet101** is most common.

Inference:

- One forward pass (inference) of ResNet50 involve **3.8 GFLOP** (floating point operations).
- Modern CPU perform at **~5.2 GFLOPs per core** (floating point operations per second).
- Modern CPU can have up to 96 cores and assuming 70% core usage, one can expect AlexNet inference to take **~8 ms** (depending on the DL software stack).
- For larger batch size like 256, core usage goes up (assume 80%). This results in **~1.6 sec**.

Training:

- Assuming the training dataset of size 50K and 20 epochs, each epoch will require 2x(50K/256) forward+backward pass. This results in **~200 minutes of training time in a single modern CPU**.

Training your model

A Convolution and Perceptron works well if the weight matrix is correct. The weight matrix is determined during the "**training**" phase of the model.

Weight matrix is specific to the training technique and the application it is trained for. These values are saved with the model details and the final model is known as "**pre-trained model**".

For training a model, a **dataset** is prepared and **backpropagation** is used.

Each loop of backpropagation is known as a **step** and on looping through all images in training dataset, it is known as an **epoch**.

Training involves multiple **epochs** (20+).

So, if there are 1024 images in training dataset and batch size is 16, then there are 64 steps in one epoch.

- Find the right epoch is important. If less epoch, then model is under-trained.
- If more epochs, then model is over-fit in which case training accuracy will be high but validation accuracy will be low.

Model should be able to learn high level features.

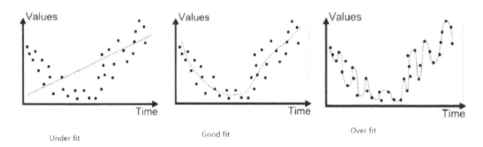

Training is a very expense in terms of computational power required. Due to this, Deep Learning did not evolve in 1980s/1990s. It was around 2010s when hardware systems matured that the training of Deep Learning models become feasible.

Inference

Inference is the process of running a **pre-trained Deep Learning model** on an actual input data on a given hardware system.

Batch size is the number of unit data that is processed by the DL model at once.

For Image Recognition models (like ResNet50, GoogleNet), the input image is of dimensions (Height x Width x Channel).

When multiple images (N) are processed together by the DL model, the **input** dimension is **Batch size x Height x Width x Channel (NHWC)**.

For one image, the **output is an array of 1000 probability values** (where the sum adds up to 1).

Note: DL models give **probability as output**. Converting it to a label or word is a software step.

For batch size N, the output is of size **N x 1000**.

1000 is for ImageNet dataset. It is the number of categories the Deep Learning model can recognize.

Datatypes (dtype) in Deep Learning

Why multiple datatypes are needed?

- Data type with lower precision will allow for numbers to be fit in a register of fixed size and SIMD instructions will work faster.
- Size of pre-trained DL model reduces.
- Training DL model with lower precision is challenging (to maintain accuracy) and different techniques exist for these.

By default, DL models are trained on FP32 (float) and inference takes place in the same dtype. Some popular dtypes are:

- BFLOAT16
- FLOAT16
- FLOAT8 (E4M3 and E5M2)
- INTEGER 8-BIT (INT8)
- INTEGER 4-BIT (INT4)

To use other dtypes, the training process changes and introduces the concept of Quantization.

Data Type	Bit Width	Format (Example)	Use Case	Performance vs FP32	Accuracy vs FP32
FP32 (Single Precision Float)	32-bit	1 sign, 8-bit exponent, 23-bit mantissa	Default for training, high precision inference	Baseline	Baseline (100%)

Format	Size	Structure	Use Case	Speedup	Precision
FP16 (Half Precision Float)	16-bit	1 sign, 5-bit exponent, 10-bit mantissa	Faster training/inference on GPUs, Mixed Precision Training (AMP)	~2× Speedup	~99% of FP32
BF16 (Brain Float 16)	16-bit	1 sign, **8-bit exponent**, 7-bit mantissa	Faster training while keeping FP32 range (TPUs, AI accelerators)	~2× Speedup	~99% of FP32
TF32 (TensorFloat-32)	19-bit	1 sign, **8-bit exponent**, 10-bit mantissa	NVIDIA Tensor Cores (FP32 range with FP16 speed)	~8× Speedup on Tensor Cores	~99% of FP32
FP8 (E4M3, E5M2)	8-bit	E4M3: 1 sign, **4-bit exponent**, 3-bit mantissa | E5M2: 1 sign, **5-bit exponent**, 2-bit mantissa	AI accelerators, FP8 training & inference	~4× Speedup	**E5M2:** 97–99% | **E4M3:** 95–98% of FP32

INT8 (8-bit Integer)	8-bit	Integer values (quantized)	Quantized inference for efficient deployment (CPUs, Edge AI, GPUs)	~4× Speedup	~95–98% of FP32
INT4 (4-bit Integer)	4-bit	Integer values (quantized)	Ultra-low precision inference (Llama3, GPTQ, Edge AI)	~8× Speedup	~85–95% of FP32
INT1 (Binary)	1-bit	{-1, 1} values	Binary Neural Networks (BNNs), extreme efficiency	~32× Speedup	~50–80% of FP32

Some insights:

- If we **add 2 INT8 numbers**, then we need 9 bits to store the output (as both INT8 inputs can be 2^8 at max so $2^8 + 2^8 = 2^9$).
- If we **multiply 2 INT8 numbers**, then we need 16 bits to store the output.
- If we **add 128 INT8 numbers**, then we need 15 bits for output (as $2^7 * 2^8 = 2^{15}$).
- **Accumulation datatype** is the datatype of the output ensuring no accuracy loss. So, for adding INT8 numbers, accumulation is in **INT16**. For dot product of two INT8 vectors, accumulation is in **INT32**.
- Not all INT32 numbers can fit in FP32. So, if **INT32 is casted to FP32, there can be accuracy loss**.

FP32 IEEE754 Floating Point

By default, input data and weights in DL model are in floating data type (FP32).

IEEE754 format is followed for FP32:

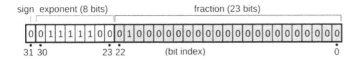

sign exponent (8 bits) fraction (23 bits)

31 30 23 22 (bit index) 0

Number = (sign) (1.M) * 2^{E-127}

127 is the **offset** to fit in a larger range of numbers.

E can range from **0** to **255**. The exponent will range from 2^{-127} to 2^{128}.

leading bit convention: Fractional part always start with 1 (that is 1.M).

Exception for 0: If E and M both are 0, it represented **positive or negative zero**.

Subnormal numbers (exception):

If E is 0, then leading bit becomes 0 and exponent is set to -126 (instead of -127).

Smallest non-subnormal number:

E = 1, M = 0, So, **$1.0 * 2^{-126}$**

Largest subnormal number:

E = 0, M = all 23 1s = 0x7FFFFF

Number: **$0.FFFFFE * 2^{-126}$**

Smallest non-zero subnormal number:

E = 0, M = 1

$0.000002 * 2^{-126}$ (very close to 0)

Special cases:

- NaN
- Positive and negative 0

Core properties due to **IEEE754** design:

- For each exponent, there is no overlap between the represented numbers.
- For each exponent, we have the same number 2^{23} of floating-point numbers.
- Within each exponent, points are equally spaced
- Larger exponents cover larger ranges, but with points more spread out.

Key insight:

- Larger integers represented by INT32 will not fit in FP32 as the integer range is less in FP32. So, **INT32 should not be casted to FP32**.

FP32 IEEE754 insights

- **Largest integer that can be stored exactly in FP32 IEEE754**

Answer is: $2^{29} - 32 = 536,870,880$

All integers beyond **536,870,880 (~536M)** results in accuracy loss. For example:

2^{29} = Actual value is 536870**12** but it is stored as 536870**900** (when converted to base 10/decimal representation) in FP32 IEEE754.

Key points:

- All integers till 2^{24} can be represented exactly
- From 2^{24} to 2^{25}, every integer with a gap of 2 can be represented exactly.
- From 2^{25} to 2^{26}, every integer with a gap of 4 can be represented exactly.
- From 2^{26} to 2^{27}, every integer with a gap of 8 can be represented exactly.
- From 2^{27} to 2^{28}, every integer with a gap of 16 can be represented exactly.
- From 2^{28} to 2^{29}, every integer with a gap of 32 can be represented exactly.
- Beyond 2^{29} (including it), no integers can be represented without error. As FP32 has only 32 bits.

In total, FP32 IEEE754 can represent exactly 2^24 + 5 * 2^23 integers = **58,720,256 (~58M) distinct integers** without any error.

Compare this with the largest integer that can be stored in INT32 datatype = 2^31 = 2,147,483,648 ~ **2.1B**

Other insights:

- In IEEE754, **NAN != NAN** (special case)
- **(x * y) / y** is not always equal to **x**. Consider the case with x = 1.0 and y = 1e-20 (very small).
- Floating-Point Arithmetic **does not follow associativity.**
  - **(x + y) + z != x + (y + z)**
- (0.1 + 0.2) != 0.3
  - As 0.1 and 0.2 cannot be represented in FP32 IEEE754 exactly leading to rounding errors.
- Sometimes, FP32 cannot detect difference between two numbers if the difference < system precision.
  - 1.0 == 1.0 + 1e-20
- **sqrt(x^2) == x** is not always true in FP32.
- **1 / (1/3) * 3 != 1** as (1/3) cannot be stored exactly in FP32.
  - Basic arithmetic rules may not hold true due to rounding errors in FP32 like: **x / y * y != x** but may hold true due to compiler level optimizations which would avoid the computation completely.

Emulate FP64 using FP32

Bit representation for **FP64** and **FP32**:

Bits	Sign S	Exponent E	Mantissa M	Bias B
FP64	1	11	53	1023
FP32	1	8	23	127

Number = (sign) (1.M) * 2^{E-B}

Due to bias, range of FP64 is significantly higher than that of FP32. Largest exponent of FP64 is 2^{1025} while for FP32, it is 2^{129}.

In DL, the goal of emulating FP64 using FP32 is to increase the precision (decimal digits) while the exponent range remains same as FP32. This helps in:

- **Higher precision arithmetic**
  - FP32 involve 23-bit mantissa which is ~7 decimal digits
  - Using 2 FP32 to emulate FP64 gives 46-bit mantissa resulting in ~14 decimal digits.
- Note the range of numbers does not increase beyond FP32.
- FP64 native support is expensive in terms of computational and power consumption.

Basic approach of emulating FP64 using FP32:

- **A = A_{high} + A_{low}**
  - A is FP64 number.
  - A_{high} and A_{low} are FP32 numbers.
  - Example: **$1.00010000056 = 1.0001 + 0.56 * 10^{-9}$**
- For addition of A and B:

- S1 = A_{high} + B_{high} [Sum of high components]
- T1 = A_{low} + B_{low} [Sum of low components]
- $S1_{error}$ = (A_{high} - S1) + B_{high} [**FP32 Rounding error in S1**]
- T2 = $S1_{error}$ + T1
- $Output_{high}$ = S1 + T2 [**Actual sum but includes new rounding FP32 error**]
- $Output_{low}$ = (S1 - $Output_{high}$) + T2 [Get the error in $Output_{high}$]
- For multiplication of A and B:

C++ code snippet emulating FP64 using FP32:

```cpp
#include <iostream>
#include <cmath>
#include <cfloat> // for FLT_EPSILON

// Structure to represent a double-double number
struct DoubleDouble {
    float hi; // High part (FP32)
    float lo; // Low part (FP32)
};

// Function to add two double-double numbers
DoubleDouble add(DoubleDouble a, DoubleDouble b) {
    DoubleDouble result;
    float s1, s2, t1, t2;

    // Add the high parts
    s1 = a.hi + b.hi;
    // Compute the error (lost bits)
    s2 = (a.hi - s1) + b.hi;

    // Add the low parts
    t1 = a.lo + b.lo;
    // Combine the results
    t2 = s2 + t1;

    // Final high and low parts
    result.hi = s1 + t2;
    result.lo = (s1 - result.hi) + t2;
```

```
        return result;
}

// Function to multiply two double-double numbers
DoubleDouble multiply(DoubleDouble a, DoubleDouble b) {
    DoubleDouble result;
    float p1, p2, p3, p4;

    // Split the numbers using Dekker's algorithm
    float c = 4097; // Splitting constant (2^12 + 1)
    float ah = a.hi * c;
    float bh = b.hi * c;
    float ah_hi = ah - (ah - a.hi);
    float ah_lo = a.hi - ah_hi;
    float bh_hi = bh - (bh - b.hi);
    float bh_lo = b.hi - bh_hi;

    // Multiply the high parts
    p1 = a.hi * b.hi;
    // Cross terms
    p2 = a.hi * b.lo;
    p3 = a.lo * b.hi;
    // Low part multiplication
    p4 = a.lo * b.lo;

    // Sum the partial products
    result.hi = p1;
    result.lo = p2 + p3 + p4;

    // Renormalize the result
    float s = result.hi + result.lo;
    result.lo = (result.hi - s) + result.lo;
    result.hi = s;

    return result;
}

// Function to print a double-double number
void printDoubleDouble(DoubleDouble x) {
    std::cout << "High: " << x.hi << ", Low: " << x.lo <<
std::endl;
}
```

```cpp
int main() {
    // Example usage
    DoubleDouble a = {1.234567f, 0.0000001234567f};
    // a = 1.234567 + 0.0000001234567
    DoubleDouble b = {2.345678f, 0.0000002345678f};
    // b = 2.345678 + 0.0000002345678

    // Addition
    DoubleDouble sum = add(a, b);
    std::cout << "Sum: ";
    printDoubleDouble(sum);

    // Multiplication
    DoubleDouble product = multiply(a, b);
    std::cout << "Product: ";
    printDoubleDouble(product);

    return 0;
}
```

Some points towards extra FP64 representation:

- Exponent range in FP64 = -1023 to 1025
- Exponent range in FP32 = -127 to 129
- 8 FP32 numbers required to maintain the exponent range of FP64.
- Mantissa: 3 FP32 numbers required to get to the lowest precision of FP64. It cannot be represented exactly.
- Given this, with 8 FP32 -> range of FP64, some accuracy loss.

FP8 in DL

There are 2 variants of FP8:

- E4M3 (for weight and activation)
- E5M2 (for gradient)

For E4M3:

- Default maximum value is **240**.
- By maintaining only one bit pattern for NaN, we get 7 extra values with maximum value being **448**.
- By reserving one pattern for 0, we get one extra value that is **480** (maximum value).

Hardware platforms for Deep Learning

Key points:

- GPUs dominate training.
- For Inference, market is divided between GPU and custom AI accelerator.
- For casual inference or on edge devices, CPU is used for inference.

Summary for different hardware platform and their suitability of training and inference of Deep Learning models:

Hardware	Notes	Best For (with Market Share)	Examples
CPU (Central Processing Unit)	Not designed for DL	**Inference (~15%)**, Not suitable for training. Limited **training (~2%)**	Intel Xeon, AMD EPYC
GPU (Graphics Processing Unit)	High parallelism with large inputs, fast matrix multiplications, high memory bandwidth and very high power consumption.	**DL training (~90%)**, inference (~50%).	NVIDIA A100, AMD MI300, RTX 4090
FPGA (Field Programmable Gate Array)	Customizable architecture, energy-efficient, low latency.	**Edge AI and real-time inference (~2%)**, low-power applications.	Xilinx Versal AI, Intel Stratix
AI Accelerator / ASIC (Application-Specific Integrated Circuit)	Optimized for AI workloads, high efficiency, low power. Vendor lock-in, high initial cost.	**Inference (~33%), training (~8%)**	Tesla Dojo, Intel Gaudi, Apple Neural Engine, Google TPU, Cerebras

| Neuromorphic Chips | Mimic brain-like computation, extremely low power. Limited software support, experimental. | **Spiking neural networks (<0.1%)**, brain-inspired AI. | Intel Loihi, IBM TrueNorth |

Accuracy

Accuracy of DL models is measured as **TopK**.

Output of DL models for tasks like Image Recognition is a list of probability for all possible categories. The output can be selected as the one with highest probability.

TopK = % of instances when the correct answer is among the top K outputs with highest probability.

Common types:

- **Top1** = Output with most probability is considered.
- **Top5** = Checks if the correct output is among the top 5 outputs with most probability.

For other tasks like **Object Detection**, the **% of correct objects** detected is considered (or if it identifies at least 5 correct objects).

For tasks like **Image Resolution**, output image is compared to the high-resolution image using **image comparison metric**.

Confusion matrix:

Prediction	TRUE	FALSE
Real label TRUE	TP	FP
Real label FALSE	TN	FN

Values:

- **TP: True positive**: Number of positive cases correctly detected by model
- **TN: True negative**
- **FP: False positive**: Number of cases wrongly labelled as positive by model
- **FN: False negative**

Popular accuracy metrics:

Metric	Formula	When?
Accuracy	Accuracy = (TP + TN) / (TP + TN + FP + FN)	Best for balanced dataset
Precision	Precision = TP / (TP + FP)	Best for cases when **FP are costly** (medical tests)
Recall / Sensitivity / True Positive Rate	Recall = TP / (TP + FN)	Best for cases when **FN is costly** (detecting cancer)
F1 score	F1 score = 2 * (Precision * Recall) / (Precision + Recall)	Best when balance between precision and recall is needed.
AOC	AOC = curve plot between Recall vs False Positive Rate (0 to 1)	Best for ranking problems: ad rank, search; 0.5 = model is random, 0.9: Model good in ranking positive samples over negative samples
NDCG (Normalized Discounted Cumulative Gain)	**DCG** = Sum(relevance score / log(rank+1); **NDCG** = DCG / ideal DCG	Best for ranking models when order matters; higher is better
MAP (Mean Average Precision)	MAP = 1/N * Sum(AP(i))	Used in retrieval + ranking problems; how well relevant items are ranked higher
RMSE (Root Mean Squared Error)	RMSE = SQRT ROOT(1/N * SUM(Ytrue - Ypred)^2)	Best when large errors should be penalized. For continuous values like housing price.
MAE (Mean Absolute Error)	MAE = 1/N * SUM(|Ytrue - Ypred|)	Best when outliers should not have too much influence, fails when large deviations matter more.

ML models will tend to maximize the selected metrics during training.

Metrics for accuracy in image classification:

Metric	Description
Top-1 Accuracy	% of times the top prediction is correct.
Top-5 Accuracy	% of times the correct label is in the top 5 predictions.

Precision / Recall / F1	Used in classification tasks to balance false positives & false negatives.

Loss

Loss is the difference between the actual output and the predicted output by the neural network.

Loss function is denoted as **J()**. As training dataset is fixed, loss function is a function on weights W of the neural network.

The goal of training a neural network is to minimize the total loss.

W' = MINIMUM{ J(W) }

Where:

- **W'** is the weight with minimum loss.
- **J()** is the loss function.
- **W** is all possible weights.

Main loss metrics used during training:

Loss Function	Best For	Example	Weaknesses
Cross Entropy Loss	Classification	Email spam detection (spam vs. not spam)	Struggles with imbalanced classes
Focal Loss	Imbalanced Classification	Fraud detection (very few fraud cases)	Requires hyperparameter tuning (γ)
Mean Squared Error (MSE)	Regression (continuous values)	Predicting house prices	Sensitive to outliers
Mean Absolute Error (MAE)	Regression (robust to outliers)	Predicting taxi fares	Not smooth for gradient descent
Huber Loss	Regression with outliers	Predicting stock prices	Needs a threshold parameter
Log-Cosh Loss	Smooth regression	Predicting sensor readings	Computationally expensive
Triplet Loss	Metric learning (distance-based models)	Face recognition (same/different person)	Needs careful triplet selection

Pairwise Ranking Loss	Ranking tasks	Search engines (rank search results)	Sensitive to hyperparameters
KL Divergence Loss	Knowledge distillation	Distilling GPT-4 into a smaller model	Assumes both distributions are well-defined
Hinge Loss (SVM Loss)	SVM Classification	Handwritten digit classification	Does not provide probability outputs
Binary Cross Entropy (BCE)	Binary Classification	Predicting whether a customer will buy or not	Can lead to vanishing gradients
Categorical Cross Entropy	Multi-class Classification	Classifying dog breeds	Sensitive to incorrect confidence calibration
CTC Loss (Connectionist Temporal Classification)	Unaligned sequence learning	Speech-to-text transcription	Computationally expensive
Dice Loss	Medical Image Segmentation	Tumor segmentation in MRI scans	Not suitable for multi-class classification
IoU (Intersection over Union) Loss	Object Detection	Detecting cars in self-driving images	Hard to optimize directly
GAN Loss (Generator & Discriminator Loss)	Generative Adversarial Networks (GANs)	Generating realistic human faces	Unstable training
Adversarial Loss (FGSM-based)	Robust ML models	Preventing adversarial attacks in image recognition	Increases training complexity

To reduce **False Positive (FP)** or **False Negative (FN)**:

Goal	Techniques	Example Use Case

Reduce FP *(Avoid wrong positives)*	• Focal Loss (focus on hard examples) • Weighted Cross-Entropy (higher penalty for FP) • Increase Decision Threshold (default 0.5 → 0.7+) • Re-ranking Model (Second-stage filtering) • Hard Negative Mining (Train on frequent FPs)	Fraud detection (avoid flagging real users)
Reduce FN *(Avoid missing positives)*	• Lower Decision Threshold (default 0.5 → 0.3) • Balanced Sampling (Oversample minority class) • Recall-Oriented Loss (FN-weighted loss) • Adversarial Training (Handle difficult edge cases) • Contrastive Learning (Better feature separation)	Medical diagnosis (avoid missing a cancer case)

Loss landscape

There are multiple weights (w0, w1, ...) and the plot of loss with all weights gives a N-dimensional plot known as **Loss Landscape**.

To minimize loss, we need to find the global minima.

This is a 2D loss landscape plot:

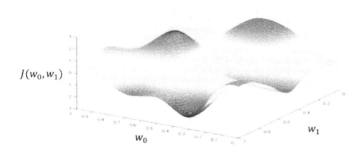

Convex functions are important and the loss landscape should be convex ideally as this helps you to find the minimum loss.

Gradient descent

Gradient descent is a method to update the weights in a neural network to minimize the loss. The steps are:

- Initialize weights randomly.
- Continue till loss with less than a threshold.
- Compute gradient. For this, compute loss and **rate of change of loss with weights** which is known as gradient.
- Update weights. $\mathbf{W_{new} = W_{old} - L \times gradient}$
  - L is the learning rate (usually around 0.01)
  - Larger L may miss the global minimum.
  - Smaller L may take a lot of time.

Backpropagation [1975]

Backpropagation algorithm is used to train neural network / perceptron and find the weights.

The idea was introduced in 1970 by Paul Werbos in his PhD thesis and was well refined for DL in 1980 by Geoffrey Hinton and others in a paper titled "Learning representations by back-propagating errors".

- **Forward Pass**: The input data is passed through the network to produce an output. This output is compared to the actual target value, and the error (loss) is calculated.
- **Backward Pass**: The error is propagated back through the network from the output layer to the input layer. This is done by **computing the gradient of the error** with respect to each weight using the *chain rule of calculus*. This tells us how much each weight in the network contributed to the error.
- **Weight Update**: Using the gradients calculated during the error propagation step, the weights are adjusted in the opposite direction of the gradient. This is usually done using an optimization algorithm like **gradient descent**. The goal is to reduce the error by making small adjustments to the weights.
- Continue the process till loss is within a limit.

Preparing dataset for training

A dataset has a large set of inputs and the corresponding set of outputs.

For a task like image recognition, the dataset will have a set of images and the corresponding label (is it a cat, dog or something else?).

A neural network is trained on the entire dataset.

The dataset is split into 3 parts:

- **Training dataset** (largest set)
- **Validation dataset** (nearly same size as test)
- **Test dataset**

Training and validation dataset is used during training. Backpropagation uses training dataset while validation dataset is used to check if training is going in correct direction.

Test dataset is used to check performance and accuracy once training is done.

Error is reported for each dataset (training error, validation error, test error).

Bias Variance

Bias = errors due to assumptions made by the DL model.

Variance = changes in DL model if the training dataset changes.

Output = F(Input) + Error(Input)

Error(Input) = Bias^2 + Variance + Irreducible Error

Goal of DL models = Low Bias + Low Variance

As we decrease bias, variance increases and vice versa.

- Under fit = High bias
- Over fit = High variance
- Good fit = Area of solutions

Visualization of bias and variance when the red circle is the actual output:

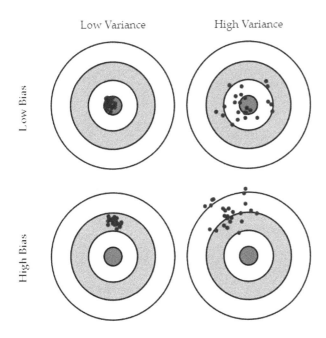

Bias is reduced using ensemble techniques like boosting.

Variance is reduced by Bagging and regularization.

Performance metrics

When the batch size is 1, then latency is measured.

Latency = time is ns to process one unit of data.

When the batch size is > 1, throughput is measured.

Throughput = images/second = Number of images processed per second.

Other metrics that one shall measure for a DL model:

Metric	Description
Memory Footprint	Total memory (RAM/VRAM) used by the model during inference.
Compute Utilization	% of GPU/TPU/CPU compute units being actively used.
Energy Efficiency	FLOPs per watt; energy consumed per inference.
Cold Start Time	Time taken to load and initialize a model before first inference.
Batch Size Scalability	How well the model scales with increasing batch size.

Metrics to be measured for training:

Metric	Description
Training Time	Time taken to train the model (hours/days).
Convergence Speed	Number of epochs required to reach optimal loss/accuracy.
GPU Utilization	Measures how effectively the GPU is being utilized (in %).
Memory Bandwidth	Data transfer speed between memory and compute units.

Communication Overhead	For distributed training, time spent on synchronization between nodes.
Gradient Noise Scale	Measures the stability of gradients (used for dynamic learning rate tuning).
Checkpointing Overhead	Time taken to save model snapshots during training.

Activation Functions

Helps DL models to learn non-linear relationships.

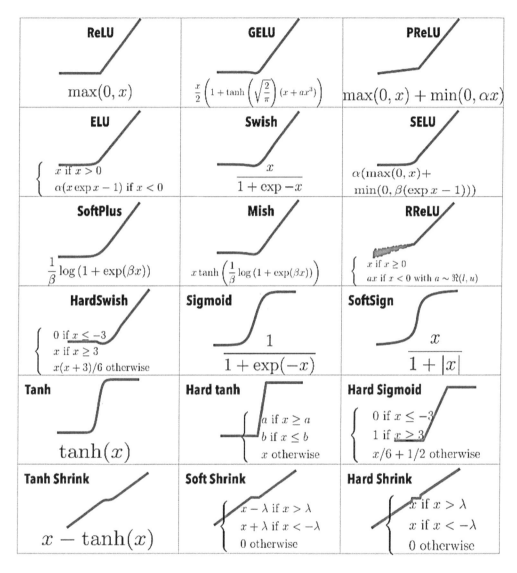

ReLU	GELU	PReLU
$\max(0, x)$	$\frac{x}{2}\left(1 + \tanh\left(\sqrt{\frac{2}{\pi}}\right)(x + ax^3)\right)$	$\max(0, x) + \min(0, \alpha x)$
ELU	**Swish**	**SELU**
$\begin{cases} x \text{ if } x > 0 \\ \alpha(x \exp x - 1) \text{ if } x < 0 \end{cases}$	$\dfrac{x}{1 + \exp -x}$	$\alpha(\max(0, x) + \min(0, \beta(\exp x - 1)))$
SoftPlus	**Mish**	**RReLU**
$\dfrac{1}{\beta} \log(1 + \exp(\beta x))$	$x \tanh\left(\dfrac{1}{\beta} \log(1 + \exp(\beta x))\right)$	$\begin{cases} x \text{ if } x \geq 0 \\ ax \text{ if } x < 0 \text{ with } a \sim \Re(l, u) \end{cases}$
HardSwish	**Sigmoid**	**SoftSign**
$\begin{cases} 0 \text{ if } x \leq -3 \\ x \text{ if } x \geq 3 \\ x(x+3)/6 \text{ otherwise} \end{cases}$	$\dfrac{1}{1 + \exp(-x)}$	$\dfrac{x}{1 + |x|}$
Tanh	**Hard tanh**	**Hard Sigmoid**
$\tanh(x)$	$\begin{cases} a \text{ if } x \geq a \\ b \text{ if } x \leq b \\ x \text{ otherwise} \end{cases}$	$\begin{cases} 0 \text{ if } x \leq -3 \\ 1 \text{ if } x > 3 \\ x/6 + 1/2 \text{ otherwise} \end{cases}$
Tanh Shrink	**Soft Shrink**	**Hard Shrink**
$x - \tanh(x)$	$\begin{cases} x - \lambda \text{ if } x > \lambda \\ x + \lambda \text{ if } x < -\lambda \\ 0 \text{ otherwise} \end{cases}$	$\begin{cases} x \text{ if } x > \lambda \\ x \text{ if } x < -\lambda \\ 0 \text{ otherwise} \end{cases}$

There are some key details:

- **ReLU** (Rectified Linear Unit): Leads to sparsity and computationally efficient.
- **Leaky ReLU**: non-zero gradient for negative inputs, solves dying ReLU problem.

135

- **PReLU** (Parametric ReLU): Variation of Leaky ReLU with learnable parameters, adapts to data during training.
- **Sigmoid**: Used in binary classification tasks, outputs in the range (0, 1).
- **Tanh** (Hyperbolic Tangent): Outputs in the range (-1, 1), centered around zero, often used in RNNs.
- **Softmax**: Used in multi-class classification tasks, ensures sum of output probabilities is 1.
- **ELU** (Exponential Linear Unit): Smooth gradient, handles negative inputs better than ReLU.
- **GELU** (Gaussian Error Linear Unit): Used in transformer architectures, approximates identity for positive inputs, smooth gradient.
- **Swish**: better performance in compared to ReLU.
- **Mish**: Smooth gradient, potential performance improvement compared to ReLU.
- **Softplus**: Smooth approximation of ReLU, avoids zero output for negative inputs.
- **SeLU** (Scaled Exponential Linear Unit): Self-normalizing activation function, maintains mean and variance of activations during training.

MaxPool and AvgPool

In Pooling operations, we have 2 inputs:

- Input image of size NxM
- Kernel size KxK only. No kernel data is provided.

The operation involves:

- For all sub-matrices of kernel size of the input image, perform the following operation:
    - Find maximum element in the sub-matrix for MaxPool.
    - Find the average of all elements in the sub-matrix for AvgPool.
    - Another operation for other pooling variants.

Pooling operation reduces the size of the input. It is used to decrease sensitivity to features, thereby creating more generalized data for better test results.

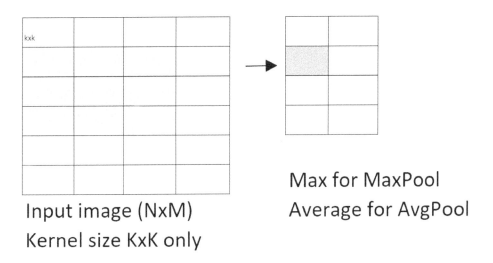

Input image (NxM)
Kernel size KxK only

Max for MaxPool
Average for AvgPool

For an image of size N^2 and kernel of size K^2, the time complexity of Pooling is **$O(N^2 K^2)$**.

Fully Connected Layer (FC)

Fully Connected (FC) layer connect all input neurons to all output neurons.

It is the last layer in a DL model and serves the following purpose:

- Set the correct number of outputs immediately.
- **Connects all the predicted features from the previous layers** to form the final output. Without this, output will depend only on a part of the input.

Previous layers perform feature extraction while **FC perform the actual classification**.

Input of previous layer = **NxM**

Weight of FC = **NxMx1000** (if model has learnt **1000 categories**)

Input is transformed as **1 x NM** and **weight** as **NM x 1000** and output is **1 x 1000**. Following FC, bias and activation is applied as well.

Dropout [1990]

The idea of dropout is inspired from brain damage. It had been observed that minor brain damage does not impact human efficiency in most cases.

Dropout is a **regularization technique** used in deep learning to prevent overfitting. During training, it randomly sets a fraction of the input units to zero at each update step, which helps prevent units from co-adapting too much. This technique forces the network to learn more robust features, as no single neuron can rely solely on the presence of other specific neurons. During inference, dropout is not applied.

Training Phase:

- Randomly select a fraction (**dropout rate**) of the neurons.
- Set the selected neurons' outputs to zero.
- Scale the remaining neurons' outputs by **1/(1−dropout rate)**.
- Proceed with forward and backward propagation using the modified outputs.

Inference Phase:

- Use the full network without dropping any neurons.
- No scaling is applied, as the weights are already adjusted during training.

DL1943 Cheatsheet: Deep Learning ©

Regularization techniques

Regularization techniques are methods to prevent overfitting by penalizing complex models.

L1 Regularization (Lasso)

- Compute the original loss (e.g., mean squared error).

$$L_{\text{lasso}} = L_{\text{original}} + \lambda \sum_i |w_i|$$

- Add the L1 penalty term, which is the sum of the absolute values of the weights multiplied by the regularization parameter λ.
- Minimize the total loss.

L2 Regularization (Ridge)

- Compute the original loss.

$$L_{\text{ridge}} = L_{\text{original}} + \lambda \sum_i w_i^2$$

- Add the L2 penalty term, which is the sum of the squared values of the weights multiplied by λ.
- Minimize the total loss.

Early Stopping

- Split the training data into a training set and a validation set.
- Train the model while monitoring the performance on the validation set.
- Stop training when the performance on the validation set starts to degrade.

Data Augmentation

- Create modified versions of the original data (e.g., rotations, translations, flips, noise addition).
- Include these augmented data points in the training set.
- Train the model on the augmented data.

Batch Normalization (BN)

- Each batch is first normalized (x-u / s) and then, scaled and shifted.
- Normalizes activations across a mini-batch to stabilize training.
- Reduces internal covariate shift, leading to faster convergence.
- Adds trainable parameters: scale (γ) and shift (β).
- Helps with gradient flow in deep networks.
- Can act as a form of regularization, reducing dependency on dropout.

Weight Sharing

- The same weight tensor is applied at different locations
- Used in CNNs (Convolutional Neural Networks) to detect patterns regardless of position.
- Reduces the number of parameters, improving efficiency and generalization.
- Common in RNNs (Recurrent Neural Networks) for sequential data processing.

Weight Constraints

- Computation: Applied as a regularization function W'=clip(W, min, max)
- Limits the values of weights to prevent instability during training.
- L2 constraint (Max-Norm): Ensures weight vectors have a fixed norm.
- Non-negativity constraint: Ensures weights remain positive, useful in some applications like NMF.

Other core DL operations

A variety of functions are performed by a variety of layers, each layer possesses its own utility and significance.

- **Input layer** - This is the layer that receives data.
- **Normalization layer** - It scales input data to suitable intervals such that bias shall be removed.
- **Convolutional layer** - This applies filters to the input such that the features maybe detected along with their locations.
- **Pooling layer** - It decreases sensitivity to features, thereby creating more generalized data for better test results.
- **Activation layer** - This applies mathematical functions f(x) to input layer, such that the ability of learning something complex and interesting is developed.
- **Dropout layer** - This layer nullifies certain random input values to generate a more general dataset and prevent the problem of overfitting.
- **Output layer** - This is the layer that produces results, devised by our neural network.

Convolution Neural Network (CNN) [1995]

Following are popular Convolution Neural Network (CNN) architectures:

AlexNet

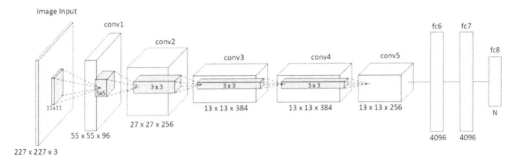

AlexNet model has **0.72 billion FLOPs**

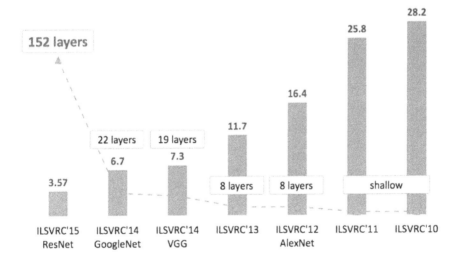

ResNet18

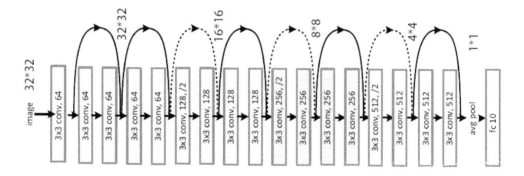

Number of parameters of different ResNet models:

- ResNet 152 model has **11.3 billion FLOP**
- ResNet 101 model has **7.6 billion FLOP**
- ResNet 50 model has **3.8 billion FLOP**
- ResNet 34 model has **3.6 billion FLOP**
- ResNet 18 model has **1.8 billion FLOP**

Where FLOP = Floating Point Operations

VGG16 (Similar to AlexNet but more number of filters) VGG19 has 19.6 billion FLOPs; VGG16 has 15.3 billion FLOPs

GoogleNet

Inception module was main contribution (9 was used).
22 layers + 12X less parameters than AlexNet. No FC layer. Only AvgPool.

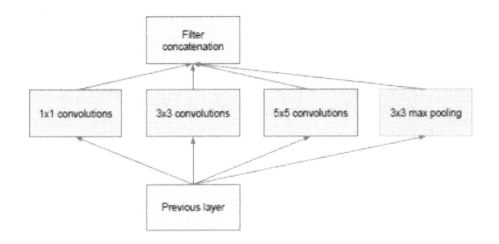

ResNet50

Residual block is the key contribution of ResNet architecture.

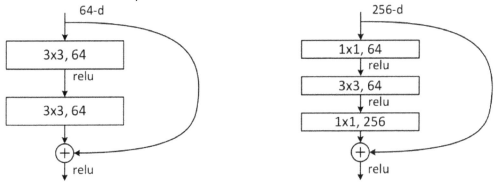

First block with 2 3x3 Conv is with ResNet18 and the 2nd block is the modified residual block for ResNet50.

MobileNet architecture

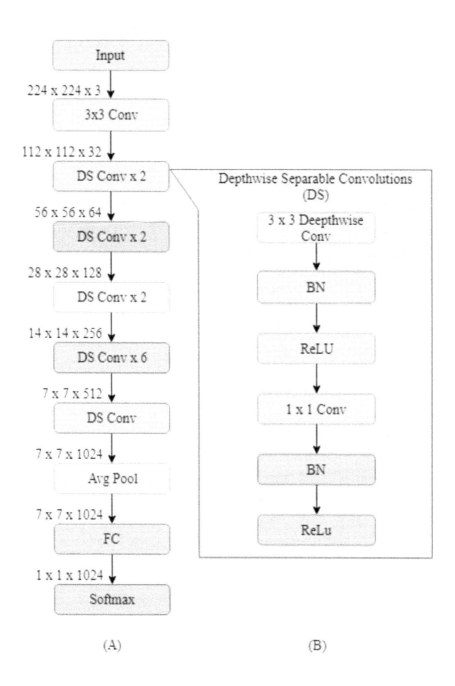

(A)

(B)

CONCLUDING NOTE

As a next step, you may randomly pick a concept from this book and dive deeper into it by researching on the topic and reading relevant research papers. If possible, work on it practically by writing code.

Remember, we are here to help you. If you have any doubts in a problem, you can contact us anytime.

Deep Learning has proved to be one of the most potential sub-domains of Computer Science. It started in 1943 and for over half a century, it did not takeoff due to hardware limitations.

When hardware was able to handle such computation overloads, the potential applications of DL became evident.

Now on completing this book, you have conquered this core domain of Deep Learning.

Be a Deep Learning Engineer.